'But God...'
The gospel in two words

Tony Bennett

DayOne

Scripture quotations marked NIV are taken from the Holy Bible, New International Version (NIV), copyright © 1973, 1978, 1984 by International Bible Society. Used by permission of Hodder & Stoughton Publishers, A member of the Hodder Headline Group. All rights reserved. "NIV" is a registered trademark of International Bible Society. UK trademark number 1448790.

Scripture quotations marked ESV are from the anglicized edition of the ESV Bible copyright © 2002 Collins, part of HarperCollins Publishers.

Scripture quotations marked NKJV are from the New King James Version (NKJV)®. Copyright © 1982 by Thomas Nelson, Inc. Used by permission. All rights reserved.

Scripture quotations marked KJV are from the Authorized (King James) Version (AV), Crown copyright.

British Library Cataloguing in Publication Data available

ISBN 978-1-84625-569-4

Published by Day One Publications
Ryelands Road, Leominster, HR6 8NZ

☎ 01568 613 740
FAX: 01568 611 473
email—sales@dayone.co.uk
web site—www.dayone.co.uk

Designed by Rob Jones, Elk Design and printed by TJ International

For my dear wife, Sue,

and in gratitude to Allan Simmons,
for his faithfulness in preaching
and his kindly encouragements
in my writing of this book,

and with much thankfulness to all the church
family at Christ Church, Westbourne

Endorsements

I have loved But God *and am looking forward to reading it again and again, and savouring its riches. I shall urge many others to get their own copy as a means to revitalizing their Quiet Times. Several of the 'but God' texts are well known, but many will not be. Each one is dealt with very faithfully in its context, with apt illustrations and quotations. As well as being wonderfully insightful for the mind, it is also profoundly helpful for the heart, with a superb choice of hymns to accompany most daily readings. Lest we rush our time of Bible study, each chapter contains questions that prompt meditation. I predict that this study of those occasions when the Bible says 'but God' will deepen our devotional lives and lead us to a more profound reverence and adoration of our Heavenly Father.*

Jonathan Fletcher, Minister, Emmanuel Church, Wimbledon, 1982–2012

Tony Bennett writes as clearly as I have heard him preach: Christ-centred, biblical, applied, along with a judicious use of anecdotes and songs, old and new, to warm the heart. And each section is topped off with excellent points for reflection. A chapter a day will help you work, rest and pray through a whole month of gospel delights! Highly recommended!

Dr Steve Brady, Principal, Moorlands College, Christchurch

In a book which will fuel your gratitude and wonder, Tony Bennett draws our attention to the many places in Scripture where our God surprises us in what he thinks, says and does. Here is the counter-intuitive God of all grace, who does do what we cannot do, and what we do not expect him to do. It's a real tonic to be reminded of this!

Alasdair Paine, Vicar, St Andrew the Great, Cambridge

Acknowledgements

I am deeply grateful to the following faithful Bible expositors and preachers for a number of the thoughts and insights developed in this book: most especially to the late James Montgomery Boice, for his expositions on Genesis, Ephesians, and the Gospels of Matthew and John; and to Dr R. Kent Hughes, for his commentaries on Genesis, Romans, as well as the Gospels of Mark and Luke. Also to Bryan Chappell, Dale Ralph Davis, Iain M. Duguid, Richard D. Phillips and Philip Graham Ryken, for their published works covering a number of the texts studied in this book. Their insights have been deeply enriching and inspiring, and I thank them most warmly. A number of the ideas in these expositions are theirs.

I am also much indebted to Dr Jonathan Griffiths, Lead Pastor of the Metropolitan Bible Church, Ottawa. Jonathan has been a true 'Barnabas' to me—'one who encourages'—first when I was new to preaching, and later when I had the germ of an idea about this book.

Finally, this book would not have been possible without the encouragement and commitment of Mark Roberts, Managing Director (UK) of Day One, to whom I am indebted for his care and professionalism throughout this project; my deepest thanks also go to my copy-editor, Suzanne Mitchell, for her wonderful eye for detail.

Contents

Foreword

'The lot is cast into the lap, but its every decision is from the LORD,' states the book of Proverbs (16:33). This was a truth that the prophet Jonah discovered for himself when the sailors on board the Tarshish-bound ship he had boarded cast lots to discover 'who is responsible for this calamity'—the ferocious storm that had suddenly engulfed them. 'And the lot fell on Jonah' (Jonah 1:7). In God's world, nothing happens by chance. The psalmist even talks of how 'all the days ordained for me were written in your book before one of them came to be' (Ps. 139:16). Many times in Scripture we see how God intervenes in the affairs of mankind. '*Nam homo proponit, sed Deus disponit*,' wrote the fourteenth-century cleric Thomas à Kempis—'For man proposes, *but God* disposes.' 'But God.' Those two words enshrine a recurring theme throughout the Scriptures of the gracious, merciful and sovereign ways in which God has intervened in the lives of men and women down the ages, and most especially in the salvation of mankind.

The idea of this book came to me whilst I was re-reading an expository commentary on Genesis written by the late Dr James Montgomery Boice (1938–2000), the much-loved senior pastor of Tenth Presbyterian Church in Philadelphia. In his exposition of Genesis 50:20—'You intended to harm me, but God intended it for good'—Boice wrote:

> I once preached a sermon series on verses of the Bible that contain the words 'but God'. There is Ephesians

2:4–5 ('But God, who is rich in mercy, for his great love wherewith he loved us, even when we were dead in sins, hath quickened us together with Christ', KJV); 1 Corinthians 2:10 ('But God has revealed it to us by his Spirit'); Romans 5:8 ('But God demonstrates his own love for us in this: While we were sinners, Christ died for us'); 1 Corinthians 10:13 ('But God is faithful, who will not suffer you to be tempted above that ye are able; but will with the temptation also make a way to escape, that ye may be able to bear it', KJV); 1 Corinthians 1:27 ('But God chose the foolish things of the world to shame the wise'); Acts 13:30 ('But God raised him from the dead'). Each of these texts depends for its effect on what goes before. Ephesians 2:4 speaks of God's love, but that is set against the background of man's sin. First Corinthians 2:10 speaks of God's revelation of Himself in His Word, but that is contrasted with our inability to know God through human measures.[1]

Martyn Lloyd-Jones (1899–1981), for almost thirty years the minister of Westminster Chapel in London, wrote in his commentary on Ephesians 2:4–5: 'These two words—"but God"—in and of themselves, in a sense contain the whole of the gospel.' They tell what God has done, how God has intervened in what otherwise was an utterly hopeless situation. The intervention of these two words and what they represent makes all the difference. Commenting on the same passage, R. C. Sproul writes:

I have always said that the first word in verse 4 is my favourite word in all the Bible. It is the word, But. As grim as the picture is [in the preceding verses] of man's fallenness, Paul hastens to add: 'But God, who is rich in mercy ...'[2]

Indeed, as these two words apply to our salvation, I would suggest that each of us, if we are truly disciples of the Lord Jesus Christ, will have experienced some kind of 'but God' moment in our lives—a time before which we were lost in our sin, but after which we could truly rejoice in God's gracious forgiveness and redemption. It may not be a Damascus Road experience like that of the Apostle Paul, but it will be a time— maybe a period of time—when you truly experienced for yourself the gracious truth of 'but God ...'

There are well over one hundred 'but God' references in the Bible, spread from the third chapter of Genesis right through to the first epistle of John. The majority of them occur in the Old Testament. Some depend upon which Bible translation one uses. Most of the texts that appear in this volume are taken from the New International Version (NIV 2011 unless flagged as 1984), but three are from the English Standard Version (ESV) and one is from the New King James Version (NKJV). In these instances the NIV has a slightly different arrangement or rendering. In this book I consider thirty-one such Scripture verses which contain the phrase 'but God', or some equivalent such as 'but Christ' or 'but Jesus', and in one case 'but the Spirit'. In many there is a sharp contrast between a dreadful, sinful human reality on the one hand, and a glorious aspect of the greatness and sovereignty of God that overcomes it.

My hope is that you might gain encouragement in our great all-powerful and all-providing God as you see how he can take the most unpromising circumstances and turn them to his glory and praise. Each chapter aims to do three things: to explain the context of the verse or passage; to explain the significance of the 'but God' intervention; and to help us to apply the truth to our own Christian lives. To quote Dr Boice once more:

> May I put it quite simply—if you understand these two words—'but God'—they will save your soul. If you recall them daily and live by them, they will transform your life completely.[3]

For to understand these two words as the Bible uses them is to understand that our salvation is truly by grace alone, through Christ alone, and that he—not we—took the initiative; or, as the hymn puts it, 'I was lost, *but Jesus* found me'![4] *Soli Deo Gloria!*

Tony Bennett

Broadstone, Dorset, 2016

God's first question

Then the man and his wife ... hid from the LORD *God among the trees of the garden.* But the LORD God *called to the man, 'Where are you?'*[1]

(Gen. 3:8–9)

T he Bible is not yet seventy verses old before we come across the first 'But God' moment. As with all of these verses, it is what comes before God's intervention that we need first of all to investigate. In Genesis chapter 2, God has placed Adam in the perfect world of the Garden of Eden (2:15) with the most permissive of rules: '*You are free* to eat from any tree in the garden; but you must not eat from the tree of the knowledge of good and evil, for when you eat from it you will certainly die' (2:16–17). This is God's reminder to Adam that he is not his own god and that he is responsible at all times to his Maker. For Adam, God knows best and knows what is for his eternal good.

But, like Adam, we think we know better. We want to run our own lives and we resent, and then reject, God's will for us. 'What is the chief end of man?' asks the first question of the *Westminster Catechism.* The answer is: 'Man's chief end is to glorify God and enjoy him forever.' But we think that our end is to gratify and enjoy *ourselves,* to bring glory to *ourselves,* and, like Adam, we quickly forget or corrupt the word of God. We readily believe the tempting sounds that say to us, 'Did God *really* say ...?' (3:1). Sin's origin is in man questioning God. The persuasive words that follow go on to directly contradict

God's declared will for us. 'You will not certainly die,' the serpent tells Eve. 'For God knows that ... you will be like God, knowing good and evil' (3:4–5). Here is Satan suggesting that God is not benevolent, and his word cannot be trusted. Eve sees, desires, takes, eats and shares—and the rest, as they say, is history: the history of fallen mankind.

And after the first sin comes the first cover-up. 'And they realised ...', says 3:7. Oh yes, they realized, but now it was all too late. So having flouted God's loving command, they now try to pull the wool over his eyes—with a fig leaf—and they try to hide. What follows is the first recorded game of hide and seek: Adam and Eve hide, and God seeks. This at first might sound terrifying, and it was. Adam admits in verse 10 to being 'afraid'. But our loving Father is so gracious that even when we have slighted and disobeyed him, he comes looking for us.

This brings us to our first 'But God', and to God's first question. '*But the* LORD *God* called to the man, "Where are you?"' What a curious question for the all-knowing God to utter! Of course God knows where Adam and Eve are, so why does he ask the question? When God asks us a question, we should know that something is probably seriously wrong. He would soon ask Cain, 'Where is your brother Abel?' (4:9). When the prophet Elijah sloped off to a cave, God asked, 'What are you doing here, Elijah?' (1 Kings 19:9). It is recorded in John's Gospel that Jesus asked Peter three times, 'Do you love me?' (John 21:15–17). The purpose of God's question here is to drive home to Adam the enormity of his sin. Peter

Williams has written that God's questions 'are meant to teach us something, or to expose to us our inner selves when we are guilty of sin or disobedience'.[2] So whenever we read the Bible and come across God asking a question, our response should be, 'Is God addressing that question to me, and, if so, what am I meant to learn from it?'

This particular question calls Adam to the bar of God's justice; it is God opening the first judicial proceedings. The inquisition is followed by the verdict and the sentence. But how gracious is the sentence! Yes, the woman will have pain in childbearing (3:16) and the man will live by the sweat of his brow (3:17–18). But physical death—the promised punishment—is postponed, a suspended sentence, as sometimes in our courts today. And when the penalty was finally exacted, it was done so, not in the Garden of Eden on the first Adam and his wife, but in another garden and on the Second Adam. It was the Lord Jesus Christ—the Messiah first promised here in verse 15—who bore the punishment for Adam and Eve's sin. And when you and I are in Christ, by faith, then he has paid the penalty for your sin and for mine.

So what are we meant to learn from God's first question? Are we like Adam and Eve, trying to hide *from* God, or have we come to the foot of the cross, trusted him for complete forgiveness, and are we now hiding *in* God's dearly beloved Son? 'For God so loved the world that He gave His only begotten Son, that whoever believes in Him should not perish but have everlasting life' (John 3:16, NKJV). Then, but only then, can we join with all the saints in singing:

> Oh, safe to the Rock that is higher than I,
> My soul in its conflicts and sorrows would fly;
> So sinful, so weary, Thine, Thine would I be;
> Thou blest Rock of Ages, I'm hiding *in* Thee.[3]

FOR FURTHER READING: GENESIS 3:1–24

Reflect on these points

1. *Like Adam, we think we know better than God. We want to run our own lives and we resent, and then reject, God's will for us.*

2. *But our loving Father is so gracious that even when we have slighted and disobeyed him, he comes looking for us.*

3. *When the penalty was finally exacted, it was done so, not in the Garden of Eden on the first Adam and his wife, but in another garden and on the Second Adam.*

4. *Are you like Adam and Eve, trying to hide from God, or have you come to the foot of the cross, trusted him for complete forgiveness, and are you now hiding in God's dearly beloved Son?*

Remembering

Only Noah was left, and those with him in the ark. The waters flooded the earth for a hundred and fifty days. But God remembered Noah ...

(Gen. 7:23–8:1)

Sin entered the world at the start of Genesis 3 and by chapter 6 verse 11 we find that 'all the people on earth had corrupted their ways'. Sin spreads. And so, at God's instruction, 'righteous' Noah built an ark in which he and his family would be saved. Truly this was an act of faith on Noah's part. Sceptics think of faith in terms of 'believing six impossible things before breakfast'. But biblical faith is 'confidence in what we hope for and assurance about what we do not see' (Heb. 11:1). Noah exhibited this kind of faith by acting on God's warning of a coming flood, even though the event of which God spoke was as yet unseen. Noah's neighbours ridiculed him, but by his faithful life Noah 'condemned the world' around him and, through faith, 'became [an] heir of the righteousness that is in keeping with faith' (Heb. 11:7). But now the waters were rising and 'only Noah was left, and those with him in the ark' (Gen. 7:23).

But God remembered Noah—the Bible's second 'But God' moment when God came to intervene in what would otherwise have been mankind's hopeless catastrophe. Not, of course, that God had ever *forgotten* Noah, but God was to show him a special sign of his remembrance. And what a truly gracious thing it is to be 'remembered' by God! Later in

Genesis we are told that God 'remembered Abraham' (19:29) and that he 'remembered Rachel', Jacob's wife (30:22), and in so doing 'enabled her to conceive'. The same phrase is used for the same purpose in 1 Samuel 1:19–20: 'the LORD remembered' Hannah, so that in due course she gave birth to Samuel. David, in Psalm 25, prays to God, 'remember me, for you, LORD, are good' (25:7). We are fully assured by Scripture that God never forgets his children, even though at times they accuse God of being forgetful. 'But Zion said, "The LORD has forsaken me, the Lord has forgotten me,"' we hear in the prophecy of Isaiah (49:14). But what follows immediately is God's promise: 'Can a mother forget the baby at her breast and have no compassion on the child she has borne? Though she may forget, I will not forget you!' (v. 15).

But how frequently we forget God! How many days pass in which, except at our specific times of prayer, it can be said of us that 'in all [our] thoughts there is no room for God' (Ps. 10:4b). Yet we say that we love God. We do not normally have to be told to think of the objects of our true love. No; our forgetfulness of God is one of the many sad and condemning proofs of our lack of love for him. We need to pray that God would truly give us an appreciation of our 'creation, preservation, and all the blessings of this life; but above all of His inestimable love in the redemption of the world by our Lord Jesus Christ; for the means of grace, and for the hope of glory'.[1] It is by thinking of these things that, by God's grace, even our hard hearts may be brought to love and adore the one who ever remembers his children.

And remembering is at the heart of the gospel. Cast your mind back to the scene at Calvary as Christ was crucified between two thieves. Luke records that one of the criminals turned to Jesus and asked, 'Remember me when you come into your kingdom' (23:42). And Jesus replied, 'Truly I tell you, today you will be with me in paradise' (23:43). How could that be? How can sinful men and women—even condemned criminals—be admitted into paradise? Well, that has something to do with what God does *not* remember about those who put their faith in the death of the Lord Jesus Christ. For God says to such as those, 'I, even I, am he who blots out your transgressions, for my own sake, and remembers your sins no more' (Isa. 43:25). But lest we think we can, like the thief in the gospel, wait until our dying hour, the Old Testament Preacher exhorts us to 'Remember your Creator *in the days of your youth*, before the days of trouble come' (Eccles. 12:1). Of course, it is never too late to turn to Christ, any more than it's ever too late to get married. But surely true love would be in doubt if a woman, upon being asked by her beloved, 'Will you marry me?', replied that she would do so, but not until she was about to die! Likewise if the man said he would propose, but not until he was on his deathbed!

Someone once remarked that the Christian life 'is a combination of amnesia and déjà vu'. We will often need to say to ourselves, 'I know I've forgotten this before.' We keep learning what we keep forgetting. So after turning to Christ as Saviour, remembering remains at the heart of the true Christian's life. 'And [Jesus] took bread, gave thanks and broke it, and gave it to them, saying, "This is my body given for you; do this *in remembrance* of me"' (Luke 22:19).

> So may our hearts remember yet
> That cross where love and justice met,
> And find in Christ our fetters freed,
> Whose mercy answers all our need:
> Who lives and reigns, our risen Lord,
> Where justice sheathes her righteous sword.[2]

For further reading: Genesis 8:1–22

Reflect on these points

1. *God never forgets his children, even though at times they accuse God of being forgetful.*

2. *How frequently we forget God! Yet we say that we love him. We do not normally have to be told to think of the objects of our true love. No; our forgetfulness of God is one of the many sad and condemning proofs of our lack of love for him.*

3. *How can sinful men and women—even condemned criminals—be admitted into paradise? That has to do with what God does* not *remember about those who put their faith in the death of the Lord Jesus Christ.*

God sees

... You would surely have sent me away empty-handed. But God *has seen my hardship.*

(Gen. 31:42)

With the connivance of his mother Rebekah, Jacob had stolen his brother Esau's blessing and, fearful of his brother's revenge, was forced to leave his home and stay with his Uncle Laban in Paddan Aram. Here he fell in love with Laban's younger daughter Rachel and worked for seven years for Laban to win the right to marry her. But Laban tricked him into marrying the elder daughter, Leah. At the cost of another seven years' work, Jacob gained the hand of his beloved Rachel in marriage. Jacob's family grew and, over the next six years, so did his prosperity in terms of cattle; and Laban's own sons became jealous. So Jacob was forced into another midnight flight—this time from his uncle's family. But unlike the flight from Esau, which was another of his mother's schemes, this departure was God's plan. 'Then the LORD said to Jacob, "Go back to the land of your fathers and to your relatives, and I will be with you"' (Gen. 31:3). But Laban pursued his nephew and there followed a verbal confrontation between the two, in which Jacob issued his litany of grievances against his uncle:

> It was like this for the twenty years I was in your household. I worked for you fourteen years for your two daughters and six years for your flocks, and you changed my wages ten times. If the God of my father, the God of Abraham and the Fear of Isaac, had not

been with me, you would surely have sent me away empty-handed (31:41–42).

There are times in our lives too when we think things are just so unfair. We really do deserve better from our fellow human beings, and from God. The result is discouragement. Like Jacob: many years after this incident—when he had lost Joseph and was then deprived of Simeon held hostage in Egypt (by Joseph!)—Jacob uttered these words used surely by us all: 'Everything is against me!' (42:36). Or like Elijah on Mount Horeb, we tell God, 'I am the only one left, and now they are trying to kill me too' (1 Kings 19:14). I think we are all prone to the Elijah complex—or, as in Genesis 42, the Jacob complex. And like Jacob and Elijah, if we think we've been especially faithful and obedient to God, we feel all the more let down. 'How can God do this to me, after all I've done?'

But when we start talking like this, we have clearly lost sight of two attributes of God—his omniscience and his grace. On this occasion, Jacob had remembered God's gracious and all-seeing intervention in his life, for, having wound himself up into something of a frenzy of self-righteousness in the previous verses, he now acknowledges God's eye upon him for good, telling Laban that 'you would surely have sent me away empty-handed. *But God* has seen my hardship and the toil of my hands, and last night he rebuked you.' Indeed God had, appearing to Laban in a vision the night before he set off to pursue Jacob's entourage and warning him 'not to say anything to Jacob, either good or bad' (Gen. 31:24).

Scripture is replete with reminders of God's all-seeing eye. In Genesis 16 we read of Hagar, having fled from Sarai's mistreatment, being found by the angel of the Lord by a desert well. Hagar names the well Beer Lahai Roi, which means 'the well of the Living One who sees me' (Gen. 16:14). When addressing the children of Israel on the merits of the Promised Land, Moses describes it as a land where 'the eyes of the LORD your God are continually on it from the beginning of the year to its end' (Deut. 11:12). King David tells us 'that the eyes of the LORD are on the righteous' (Ps. 34:15), whilst his son Solomon has this reminder of the fact that God is all-seeing: 'The eyes of the LORD are everywhere, keeping watch on the wicked and the good' (Prov. 15:3).

And what is true of the Father is true also of his Son. When Nathanael is brought to Jesus by Philip, he is staggered that Jesus seems to know him: 'How do you know me?' he asks Jesus somewhat incredulously. Jesus answers, 'I saw you while you were still under the fig-tree before Philip called you' (John 1:48). This one simple fact causes Nathanael to confess that Jesus is 'the Son of God ... the king of Israel' (v. 49).

It is both reassuring and challenging to realize that God sees us and, as a consequence, knows all there is to know about us. Just as it was for Jacob, confronted by Laban in the hill country of Gilead, it is wonderfully reassuring for us to know that, as the nineteenth-century hymnwriter James Wallace puts it, 'There is an eye that never sleeps.' But it is also challenging because I take great care to conceal my sinfulness from those around me, but it is quite impossible to conceal it from him who sees me. Bishop Ken rightly reminds us in one of his hymns to 'Think how all-seeing God thy ways / and all thy secret thoughts surveys'.[1] Let us therefore make it our daily prayer to live each moment for him—the Living One who sees me.

> We have not feared Thee as we ought,
> Nor heeded Thine all-seeing eye,
> Nor guarded word and deed and thought,
> Rememb'ring that our God was nigh.
> Lord, give us faith to know Thee near
> And grant the grace of holy fear.[2]

FOR FURTHER READING: GENESIS 31

Reflect on these points

1. *There are times when we think things are just so unfair. If we think we've been especially faithful and obedient to God, we feel all the more let down. But Scripture is replete with reminders of God's all-seeing eye.*

2. *And what is true of the Father is true also of his Son. God sees us and knows all there is to know about us.*

3. *This is also challenging: it is quite impossible to conceal my sinfulness from him who sees me.*

God with us

And Joseph's master took him and put him into the prison ... But the LORD *was with Joseph and showed him steadfast love ... And whatever he did, the* LORD *made it succeed.*

(Gen. 39:20–23, *ESV)*

Success in prison may seem an unlikely concept. None of us would willingly choose to go to prison. But for Joseph—as for some other Bible characters—prison strengthened both his faith and his character. For the prophet Jeremiah, prison strengthened his witness. For the Apostle Paul, it was during his prison years that he wrote Philippians, Colossians, 2 Timothy and Philemon. And the Apostle John was a prisoner on the island of Patmos when he was inspired by the Holy Spirit to write the climactic book of the Bible. More recently, John Bunyan (1628–1688) conceived of *Pilgrim's Progress* during his first term of imprisonment in Bedford County Gaol and completed the work during his second term. Much more recently, one evening in January 1975, Watergate conspirator Charles Colson prayed from his prison cell in Alabama: 'Lord, I praise you for leaving me in prison. I praise you for giving me your love ... for just letting me walk with Jesus.'[1] How tempted we can be to think that, when our circumstances are hard, God has deserted us.

Joseph had been sold by his brothers to Midianite merchants (Gen. 37:28) and had ended up as a slave in Egypt in the household of Potiphar. He had been wrongly imprisoned by Potiphar after being maliciously accused by Potiphar's wife of attempted rape. The truth was that she had wanted to get Joseph into bed with her and he had refused, running out of the house to get away from her (39:11–13). So here at the end of chapter 39, Joseph is languishing as an Israelite in an Egyptian prison. Surely many of us in similar circumstances would have been tempted to conclude that God had forsaken us—and all this after Joseph had *resisted* temptation. Might it not have been natural for Joseph to think that, had he gone to bed with his master's wife, life might have turned out rather better?

But the inspired writer informs us that, yes, Joseph's outward circumstances did indeed look bleak, '*but the* LORD was with Joseph and showed him steadfast love'. God was to use Joseph's time in prison to mould him into the role of the godly leader that God was calling him to be. Stony Brook, a private Christian school on Long Island, New York, has as its motto, 'Character Before Career'. What this is suggesting to its students is that character—integrity, morality and godliness—is a prerequisite for walking with God and being used by him in whatever career one enters. It could have been Joseph's motto in prison: character before career.

When the temptation of illicit sex presented itself in the shape of Mrs Potiphar, what was Joseph's reaction? He said to her, 'How ... could I do such a wicked thing and sin *against* God?' (39:9). Then, when the king's butler and baker joined him in the gaol and told Joseph of their dreams, what was Joseph's reaction? 'Do not interpretations belong *to* God?' (40:8). And when eventually Pharaoh sent for Joseph and asked him to interpret his dreams, what was Joseph's reaction then? 'I cannot do it ... *but God* will give Pharaoh the answer he desires' (41:16). Later in his years of freedom and prosperity in Egypt, Joseph married and his first son was born. And Joseph called him Manasseh, '*because God* has made me forget all my trouble and all my father's household' (41:51). He called his second son Ephraim—and why? 'It is *because God* has made me fruitful in the land of my suffering' (41:52). And when later Joseph was reunited with the brothers who had sold him into slavery, what were Joseph's first thoughts—of revenge and anger? No. 'Do not be distressed and do not be angry with yourselves for selling me here, *because* it was to save lives that *God* sent me ahead of you' (45:5). Do you notice the pattern here? Joseph could not speak about anything without talking about his God. Things 'belong to *God*'; 'but *God* will give the answer'; '*God* has made me forget my trouble'; '*God* has made me fruitful'; '*God* sent me.' God! God! God!

As Iain Duguid points out, the danger of this episode is that we all want to emulate Joseph's resisting of temptation but without having to suffer similar consequences. But God was not at work in Joseph's life because he obeyed God and resisted temptation. Genesis 39:21 tells us that God showed Joseph *mercy*, and mercy is not earned by our good(ish) behaviour. Genesis 38 tells of Joseph's older brother Judah falling spectacularly into sexual sin. But God was merciful to Judah too. At the very start of his Gospel, Matthew tells us that the Lord Jesus was born through the line of Judah (Matt. 1:3), not Joseph. Duguid reminds us:

> Someone who sins and falls so spectacularly can still be incorporated into the people and plan of God. In the same way, God will use your sin to humble you and make you appreciate his grace in a way that you never could if he always enabled you to stand in the face of fierce temptation.[2]

'*But the* LORD was with Joseph and showed him steadfast love.' The key to our daily walk with God is to know the reality of him who was born Emmanuel—God with us—wherever God in his sovereign will places us. Do you believe that?

FOR FURTHER READING: GENESIS 39

Reflect on these points

1. *How tempted we can be to think that, when our circumstances are hard, God has deserted us.*

2. *Many of us in similar circumstances to Joseph's would have been tempted to conclude that God had forsaken us—and all this after Joseph had* resisted *temptation.*

3. *We all want to emulate Joseph's resisting of temptation but without having to suffer similar consequences. But mercy is not earned by our good(ish) behaviour.*

My weakness ...
God's strength

'I cannot do it,' Joseph replied to Pharaoh, *'but God will ...'*

(Gen. 41:16)

Whilst in prison, Joseph met Pharaoh's cupbearer and baker who had offended their master. Joseph correctly interpreted their dreams: the baker was hanged but the cupbearer was reinstated. Joseph had asked the cupbearer to mention him to Pharaoh (Gen. 40:14) 'and get me out of this prison'. But that chapter ends with three devastating words about the cupbearer: 'he forgot him.' Chapter 41 opens thus: 'When two full years had passed ...' How those years must have dragged for Joseph! Surely to begin with, every time footsteps approached his cell he must have thought, 'This is it! The cupbearer has remembered, and Pharaoh has sent for me.' But as the days turned to weeks and then to months, Joseph must have given up all hope. Bereft of obvious signs of God's mercy towards us, how often we are tempted to think that God has forgotten us!

But on this occasion, all it took to bring about God's plan for Joseph's future was for Pharaoh to have a bad dream. 'The king's heart is a stream of water in the hand of the LORD; he turns it wherever he will,' writes Solomon (Prov. 21:1, ESV). And Pharaoh's dream is the catalyst to bring about Joseph's freedom from prison. As suddenly as Joseph was transported from Potiphar's penthouse to the prison house in chapter 39, so Joseph is now propelled from the prison to the palace in chapter 41, and he is standing before Pharaoh listening to his 'I have a dream' speech.

Let's cast our minds back over Joseph's life. How did all these problems start? Wasn't it with a dream about his brothers' sheaves of grain bowing down to his sheaf (37:6–7)? And now Pharaoh wants to know what *his* dream means. Surely we would have forgiven Joseph for looking Pharaoh in the eye and saying, 'Dreams? Oh, I wouldn't have anything to do with those if I were you. I had one once and believed it, and look where it got me!'

More seriously, Joseph would have been only human to have thought twice before talking to Pharaoh—who was regarded by his subjects as a man-god—about the one true God. Surely it would have been understandable to have allowed the grandeur of the king's court to affect his speaking. Charles Colson, the one-time White House aide to President Nixon, became familiar with the way in which the President's severest critics, overawed by the surroundings of the West Wing and the Oval Office, could suddenly turn to putty in the President's hands. Baying pit bulls suddenly morphed into simpering chihuahuas. Wrote Colson:

> Invariably, the lions of the waiting room became the lambs of the Oval Office. They nodded when the President spoke, and in those rare instances when they disagreed, they did so apologetically, assuring the President that they personally respected his opinion. Ironically, none were more compliant than

the religious leaders. Of all people, they should have been the most aware of the sinful nature of man and the least overwhelmed by pomp and protocol. But theological knowledge sometimes wilts in the face of world power.[1]

Furthermore, many of us would have been tempted to have played along with Pharaoh's flattery. 'I had a dream, and *no one* can interpret it. But I have heard it said of *you* that when *you* hear a dream *you* can interpret it,' says Pharaoh to Joseph (41:15). 'Well, yes, now you come to mention it, Your Majesty, I am rather a whizz with dreams. You've probably heard that I was right on the money with both your baker and cupbearer.' No! Not Joseph. Joseph was humbly dependent upon God and even after years of disappointment was still in the business of 'God promotion' rather than self-promotion.

'I cannot do it,' he replies—or more literally, 'it is not in me', which in the original is just a single word—an exclamation of self-deprecation. We are always stronger when, before God, we know our own weakness and his all-sufficient strength. For godly self-knowledge follows 'I cannot do it' with 'but God will'. As Thoro Harris puts it in his hymn:

> Every need His hand supplying,
> Every good in Him I see;
> On His strength divine relying,
> He is all in all to me.[2]

'On *His* strength divine relying'—but our tendency is to

boast about our own abilities, not God's. And what does that say about our hearts? It shows we don't really trust God to protect us and provide for us. It shows that we are more focused on being rated highly by those around us—especially the so-called great and the good—than by Almighty God. Why am I so consumed with anger and self-pity when folk around me—my family, my colleagues, my church minister, my friends—are not duly appreciative of my talents and accomplishments? Why aren't these folk more thankful just to have me around? But the litmus test is who I regard as my primary audience. If it's the aforementioned list, then I'm going to play to that audience and be looking for their applause and appreciation. But if God really is 'all in all to me', then I will remember, moment by moment, that God is my audience, and I will be content to live in his shadow instead of wanting to be the centre of attention myself. Then, and only then, will I be able to say with the Apostle Paul, 'But [God] said to me, "My grace is sufficient for you, for my power is made perfect in weakness." Therefore I will boast all the more gladly about my weaknesses, so that Christ's power may rest on me' (2 Cor. 12:9).

FOR FURTHER READING: GENESIS 41

Reflect on these points

1. *Bereft of obvious signs of God's mercy towards us, how often we are tempted to think that God has forgotten us!*

2. *Joseph was humbly dependent upon God and even after*

years of disappointment was still in the business of 'God promotion' rather than self-promotion.

3. *We are more focused on being rated highly by those around us than by Almighty God. But if God really is 'all in all to me', then I will remember that God is my audience, and I will be content to live in his shadow instead of wanting to be the centre of attention myself.*

God's perfect plan

But God *sent me ahead of you to … save your lives by a great deliverance. So then it was not you who sent me here,* but God.

(Gen. 45:7–8)

The story of Joseph must be one of the greatest stories ever told, and throughout it is seen God's perfect plan. Joseph was sold into slavery in Egypt and worked in Potiphar's house. But he ended up in prison, in order that he would meet Pharaoh's cupbearer, in order that he would interpret Pharaoh's dreams and thus become Egypt's prime minister, in order that the lives of his family and many others would be saved during the famine years. 'Oh, the depth of the riches of the wisdom and knowledge of God! How unsearchable his judgments, and his paths beyond tracing out!' (Rom. 11:33). How fitting that Joseph's telling of this perfect plan to his brothers—now reunited with the brother they had sold into slavery—includes not one but two 'but God' phrases.

We noted in an earlier exposition how Joseph was wonderfully God-centred in his words. Here, as he talks with his brothers who had so injured and maligned him, God is centre stage yet again: '*God* sent me ahead of you' (v. 5); '*God* sent me ahead of you' (v. 7); 'So then, it was not you who sent me here, but *God*' (v. 8); '*God* has made me lord of all Egypt' (v. 9). Nothing is more characteristic of Joseph than his ability to relate everything that has happened to him to God. By looking past the secondary causes of his seeming misfortune and instead looking to God, who is the First Cause, Joseph gains a stabilizing perspective on his troubled life and is therefore able to forgive his brothers and remain thankful to his all-providing God. Do you have such a perspective on your life? You will exhibit much less fear, grumbling and self-pity if you do. Do you hold in your mind *both* teachings taught by the Apostle James in the first chapter of his epistle: not only that 'every good and perfect gift is from above' (1:17), but also to 'consider it pure joy ... whenever you face trials of many kinds' (1:2)?

The Reverend Henry Blunt (1794–1843), one-time Rector of Holy Trinity, Upper Chelsea, loved to tell in his sermons the story of a shepherd of Salisbury Plain. When asked by an enquirer, 'What weather are we likely to have?', the shepherd would reply, 'It will be what pleases me.' 'How do you know?' asked the enquirer. 'Because,' said the shepherd, 'it will be what pleases God, and what pleases God shall please me.' Blunt would add: 'Few would be the complaints of the Christian if this feeling reigned in the heart: very rare indeed are the grumblings where God's will is our will, and God's pleasure, our pleasure.'[1] Joseph had indeed learnt to say on all occasions and in all circumstances, 'what pleases God shall please me'. This is the mind of the faithful child of God, of the one who truly trusts God to be sovereign. Is it your mind?

In 1978, Harold Kushner, a Boston rabbi, wrote a book entitled *When Bad Things Happen to Good People*. It was an instant success and appeared on the *New York Times* bestseller list for a year. But its thesis was that God is all-loving but not all-powerful; good but not sovereign. So when bad things happen to 'good people'—whoever *they* are—it is because events are out of God's control. In such circumstances, argued Kushner, we have to 'learn to love [God] and forgive him despite his limitations'. This may provide an easy solution to the problem of evil and suffering, but it has absolutely nothing to do with the God of the Bible. Kushner clearly hadn't noticed Job's declaration, 'The LORD gave, and the LORD has taken away; blessed be the name of the LORD' (Job 1:21, NKJV). God had a purpose in Job's suffering, just as he had in Joseph's, and just as he has in your suffering and in mine. With God, nothing is accidental, and nothing is outside his control. Have you learnt to say to God with Job: 'I know that you can do all things; no purpose of yours can be thwarted' (Job 42:2)?

Writing in his autobiography, John Newton, the former slave trader and then gospel minister, had this to say of God's plan for his life:

> But to us there is a time coming when our warfare shall be accomplished, our views enlarged, and our light increased. With what transports of adoration and love shall we look back upon the way by which the Lord led us! We shall then see and acknowledge that mercy and goodness directed every step; we shall see that what our ignorance once called adversities and evils, were in reality blessings which we could not have done well without. Nothing befell us without a cause; no trouble

came upon us sooner or pressed on us more heavily, or continued longer than our case required. Our many afflictions were, each in their place, among the means employed by divine grace and wisdom to bring us to the possession of that exceeding and eternal weight of glory which the Lord has prepared for His people.[2]

God wants us to know that he is in charge; that he has a perfect plan for our lives; that in *all* circumstances he is sovereign. He wants us to learn the lesson of these words of Joseph and benefit from them. And the lesson can be summed up in four words: 'God ... God ... God ... God.'

FOR FURTHER READING: GENESIS 45:1–15

Reflect on these points

1. *By looking past the secondary causes of his seeming misfortune and instead looking to God, who is the First Cause, Joseph gains a stabilizing perspective and is therefore able to forgive his brothers and remain thankful to his all-providing God. Do you have such a perspective on your life?*

2. *Joseph had learnt to say on all occasions and in all circumstances, 'what pleases God shall please me'. This is the mind of the faithful child of God. Is it your mind?*

3. *God had a purpose in Job's suffering, just as he had in Joseph's, and just as he has in your suffering and in mine. With God, nothing is accidental, and nothing is outside his control.*

Looking back …
looking forward

Then Israel said to Joseph, 'I am about to die, but God will be with you.'

(Gen. 48:21)

The phrase 'famous last words' has two meanings. In 1962, a spokesman for Decca Records commented that 'the Beatles have no future in show business'. More recently, in 2007, the CEO of Microsoft, Steve Ballmer, stated categorically that 'there's no chance that the iPhone is going to get any significant market share—no chance'. In the light of the success of both the Beatles and the iPhone one might say that these were 'famous last words', in the sense that they were words that proved to be woefully and ironically incorrect. In a different sense, the famous last words of the English politician and writer Joseph Addison (1672–1719) were these: 'See in what peace a Christian can die.' Well, here in Genesis 48 we have Jacob's famous last words—in the latter sense.

Since our last study, Jacob (Israel) has travelled to Egypt to be reunited with his son Joseph (ch. 46) and has met with Pharaoh (ch. 47). Now in chapter 48 the old man Jacob is ready to bless Joseph's two sons, Manasseh and Ephraim. Back in chapter 27, when Jacob's ageing and near-blind father Isaac tried to bless his favourite son, Esau, against God's declared instructions, Jacob tricked Isaac into blessing him instead. So we are glad to see there is going to be no trickery this time. But there is to be another divinely inspired reversal: Ephraim the younger is to be preferred over Manasseh the elder, as with

Jacob and Esau. The inspired writer shows clearly Joseph's careful choreography to ensure there is no mistake, given Jacob's failing eyesight: Ephraim is on the right to be blessed by Jacob's left hand; Manasseh is on the left to be blessed by Jacob's right hand (48:13). But then the old man crosses his arms! Joseph is angry and tries to 'correct' his father. 'But his father refused and said, "I know, my son, I know" ... So he put Ephraim ahead of Manasseh' (vv. 19–20). And Joseph immediately submits. God's choice it is, and God's choice for Joseph was final. It always had been—whether at home, in Potiphar's household, in prison or in Pharaoh's court. But why Ephraim and not Manasseh? Why does God show his love and mercy to one more abundantly than to another, or even instead of another? The Bible gives the answer when Moses is explaining to the children of Israel why God had loved them:

> The Lord did not set his affection on you and choose you because you were more numerous than other peoples, for you were the fewest of all peoples. But it was because the Lord loved you (Deut. 7:7).

Don't you just love God's logic? He loves us—why? Because he loves us. That's what God's free grace is—totally and completely undeserved.

Having blessed Joseph's sons, Jacob then prepares to pass on the baton of faith. 'Then Israel said to Joseph, "I am about to die, *but God* will be with you"' (v. 21a). Charles Haddon Spurgeon once preached a sermon in which he linked this text to three previous references to God's presence in Jacob's story.

In Genesis 28, Jacob was forced to leave home because of Esau, and God appeared to Jacob at Bethel to tell him, 'I *am* with you' (28:15). In Genesis 31, God appeared again to Jacob, this time to send him home after his twenty years with Laban, and assured him, 'I *will be* with you' (31:3). Two verses later, whilst he is reflecting on God's blessings during those twenty years, Jacob states, 'God ... *has been* with me' (31:5). Present, future and past—Jacob knew God's presence and faithfulness in all three. Now he passes on the baton of faith to the next generation. God has been with *me*, Jacob thinks, so now on his deathbed he assures Joseph, 'God will be with *you*.'

As we grow older, can we look back with thankfulness and proclaim, 'God *has been* with me'? Remember, too, that God was with Jacob despite his faults and failures. And he will be with us despite our faults and failings if we have truly trusted in his Son for forgiveness. An older Christian should, like Jacob, be able to look back on his or her life and testify to the comforting presence of God. This is how Spurgeon put it:

> If you trust God, this will be the verdict at the close of life. When you come to die you shall look back upon a life which has not been without its trials and its difficulties, but you shall bless God for it all.[1]

As the psalmist so beautifully puts it, 'Return to your rest, my soul, for the LORD has been good to you' (Ps. 116:7).

But Jacob looks not only back but forward, and so should we. We should look forward when we are older: entrusting our children, our grandchildren, nephews and nieces to the God whom we have trusted. 'I may be about to die,' we may say, 'but God will be with you.' Or maybe you are that younger relative and you are wondering whether the God who so wonderfully provided for your father, mother, uncle or aunt can provide for you. You know the answer: God is almighty, and he is unchanging. He is the God of Abraham, the God of Isaac and the God of Jacob—and of Joseph, Ephraim and Joshua. He will be with you just as he was with the saints of old. 'Jesus Christ is the same yesterday and today and for ever' (Heb. 13:8). Hallelujah!

> So Spirit, come, put strength in every stride,
> Give grace for every hurdle.
> That we may run with faith to win the prize
> Of a servant good and faithful.
> As saints of old still line the way,
> Retelling triumphs of His grace,
> We hear their calls, and hunger for the day
> When with Christ we stand in glory.[2]

FOR FURTHER READING: GENESIS 48

Reflect on these points

1. *God loves us—why? Because he loves us. That's what God's free grace is—totally and completely undeserved.*

2. *As we grow older, we should be able to look back with thankfulness and proclaim, 'God has been with me', despite our faults and failings.*

3. *We should also look forward, entrusting our children, grandchildren, nephews and nieces to the God whom we have trusted.*

4. *Or maybe you are wondering whether the God who so wonderfully provided for previous generations can provide for you. The answer is: God is almighty, and he is unchanging.*

God working
for our good

You intended to harm me, but God *intended it for good.*

(Gen. 50:20)

In the 1949 film *Red Light*, Raymond Burr (better known for his later portrayals of detectives Perry Mason and Robert T. Ironside) plays a crook, Nick Cherney, who has been imprisoned for embezzling money from Johnny Torno's trucking company. To get back at Johnny, Nick arranges for Johnny's brother, Jess—a heroic chaplain just returned from the Second World War—to be murdered in a hotel room. When Johnny arrives at the hotel room just after Jess has been shot, he hears Jess's dying words to him, which are simply, 'It's in the Bible.' Johnny eventually realizes that Jess was referring to the Gideon Bible in the hotel room and, believing that his brother may have written a clue as to his murderer's identity within its covers, tracks down the Bible. What Johnny finds, however, is that his brother had circled the verse Romans 12:19—'Vengeance is mine; I will repay, saith the Lord' (KJV)—a dying plea to his brother not to take revenge against his killer. To cut a long (eighty-three-minute) story short, the film ends with a fight between Nick and Johnny on the rooftop of the trucking firm, which ends when, in the midst of an intense rainstorm, Nick steps on the main power cable to the firm's huge roof neon name sign and is electrocuted. The film closes with Johnny standing over Nick's dead body, reciting the verse from Romans, and looking up at the still-illuminated lower part of the neon sign, which is still flashing and reads

'24-hour service'. It must be one of Hollywood's best pieces of biblical illustration!

By the final and fiftieth chapter of Genesis, Jacob is dead, and Joseph's brothers are fearful of reprisals. 'What if Joseph holds a grudge against us and pays us back for all the wrongs we did to him?' they muse (50:15). One can fully understand why Joseph might be feeling vengeful. He has suffered not only from the hatred of his brothers, but also from the lies of an influential woman (Potiphar's wife, 39:17–18), wrongful imprisonment (39:20) and the forgetfulness of a friend (Pharaoh's cupbearer, 40:23). After the cupbearer's release from prison, we are told that 'two full years ... passed' before Joseph's own release (41:1). One can well understand the brothers' fears.

So they send word to Joseph to implore his forgiveness. Notice that they are too fearful to appear in person. The emissary is to say to Joseph, '"I ask you to forgive your brothers the sins and the wrongs they committed in treating you so badly." Now please forgive the sins of the servants of the God of your father' (50:17). We are then told that the brothers came and 'threw themselves down' in front of Joseph, declaring 'we are your slaves' (v. 18). So how would you and I have replied? 'Slaves? What do you mean, slaves? Slavery is too good for you! You can all go and cool your heels in the same prison I had to endure, and for double the time!' But Joseph's reply? 'Don't be afraid. Am I in the place of God? You intended to harm me, *but God* intended it for good' (vv. 19–20).

We need to notice two things about Joseph's reply. First, Joseph shows what it means to forgive. There is no pussyfooting around. The brothers said they 'did evil' (v. 17, ESV). Joseph agrees—'you meant evil' (v. 20, ESV). We need to call sin, sin, and evil, evil. Doing so will help us to see the awfulness of our sin, in the sight both of others and of God. If you want to see what that sounds like, read Psalm 51. How do *our* confessions sound? Do we just say 'sorry' to God, or do we 'earnestly repent' of our sins because 'the memory of them grieves us' and 'the burden of them is more than we can bear'?[1] True, it is the heart more than the lips that is most indicative of our appreciation of sin's severity, but our lips will often reflect what is in our hearts.

Second, these verses show clearly that evil deserves punishment. When Joseph tells his brothers 'Don't be afraid', it's not because what the brothers did was no big deal. Rather, by adding, 'Am I in the place of God?' Joseph acknowledges God to be the rightful judge. 'Vengeance is mine; I will repay, saith the Lord.' Thus these verses speak to our need of forgiveness, and to face up to the reality of our sin.

So how could Joseph make such a gracious reply to his brothers? Surely it was because he knew the twin truths of God's sovereignty and God's goodness. God was able to overrule the evil intended by the brothers to eventually bring about good in Joseph's life. 'You meant evil ... *but God* meant good.' As we read elsewhere in the Old Testament: '"For I know the plans I have for you," declares the LORD, "plans to prosper you and not to harm you, plans to give you hope and a future"' (Jer. 29:11). In the New Testament, Luke gives us another 'but God' moment as he narrates Stephen's address to the Sanhedrin: 'Because the patriarchs were jealous of Joseph, they sold him as a slave into Egypt. *But God* was with him' (Acts 7:9).

And what is the example of the greatest evil being turned to the greatest good? Surely it is the cross upon which our Lord Jesus Christ offered himself as a full, perfect and sufficient sacrifice for the sins of all who would trust in him. It is at the cross that we see evil being judged in the person of Jesus, the only completely innocent person who ever lived, God thereby declaring the guilty pardoned. Just as Joseph's brothers struggled to believe that Joseph had truly forgiven them, so we often struggle to grasp God's forgiveness for us. But 'If we confess our sins, [God] *is* faithful and just and *will* forgive us our sins and purify us from *all* unrighteousness' (1 John 1:9). It's in the Bible—and it's a twenty-four-hour service!

FOR FURTHER READING: GENESIS 50

Reflect on these points

1. *How do our confessions sound? While it is our hearts more than our lips that best indicate our appreciation of sin's severity, our lips will often reflect what is in our hearts.*

2. *Joseph could make such a gracious reply to his brothers because he knew the twin truths of God's sovereignty*

and God's goodness. God was able to overrule the evil intended by the brothers to eventually bring about good in Joseph's life.

3. *The greatest evil was turned to the greatest good at the cross upon which our Lord Jesus Christ, the only completely innocent person who ever lived, offered himself as a full, perfect and sufficient sacrifice for the sins of all who would trust in him.*

Not judging by appearances

People look at the outward appearance, but the LORD *looks at the heart.*

(1 Sam. 16:7)

'I thought him about the ugliest man I had ever seen.' So said someone upon meeting Abraham Lincoln two years before he was elected President of the United States of America. One doubts whether Lincoln could be elected President today. For that matter, how about Franklin Roosevelt, who was confined to a wheelchair from the age of thirty-nine? For we live in an age where image counts for much. Packaging, good looks, reputation and charisma are what we look for in our leaders.

Nothing much has changed since Old Testament times. Israel's first king, Saul, is introduced to us as 'as handsome a young man as could be found anywhere in Israel, and he was a head taller than anyone else' (1 Sam. 9:2). Saul, however, turned out to be a disastrous leader, and within the space of seven chapters God had 'rejected him as king over Israel' (16:1). So the prophet Samuel is sent in search of Saul's successor—to Jesse of Bethlehem, for God tells Samuel that he has chosen one of Jesse's sons to be the new king.

One might think that, after the fiasco of head-and-shoulders-above-everyone-else Saul, Samuel would be a bit wary of 'looks'. But Samuel is human, and in verse 6 we read, 'Samuel saw Eliab and thought, "Surely the LORD's anointed stands here before the LORD."' As Dale Ralph Davis comments:

> Eliab was doubtless an impressive hulk of manhood.
> Around 6'2" perhaps, about 225 pounds, met people
> well, excellent taste in aftershave lotion, and so on.
> Perhaps he'd starred for the Bethlehem High School
> football team.[1]

Samuel pretty much has the anointing oil in his hand when the biblical narrative interjects: '*But the* LORD said to Samuel ...' Thankfully, Samuel is not left to his own devices. God interposes and saves Samuel—and Israel—from another disastrous choice. '*But the* LORD said to Samuel, "Do not consider his appearance or his height, for I have rejected him. The LORD does not look at the things people look at. People look at the outward appearance, *but the* LORD looks at the heart."'

Our lives, like Samuel's, are full of choices: whom to include in our close circle of friends; whom to appoint to posts of Christian leadership; for some, whom to marry. Will our choices be governed by externals or internals? Will our choices be governed by the sight of our eyes or by the thoughts of God's heart? For as God reminds us through the prophet Isaiah, 'My thoughts are not your thoughts' (Isa. 55:8). How is the basis of God's choice different from ours?

First, God's choice is contrary to human reason. 'Surely this is the one,' Samuel is saying in verse 6 when he sees Eliab. He probably said it six more times as Abinadab (v. 8), Shammah (v. 9) and four more of Jesse's sons were paraded in front of him (v. 10). 'The LORD has not chosen these,' Samuel finds himself saying to Jesse. 'Are these all the sons you have?' 'Oh, there's the boy David,' we can hear Jesse saying, almost apologetically, 'but he's out with the sheep.' The one no one even thought of mentioning. And what do we find? '*He* is the one,' says the Lord to Samuel in verse 12. For God is more concerned with a pure heart than with pure looks. That's why God's choices are contrary to human reason. He's more concerned with character than with reputation. And what is character? It's what God knows we are when we know there's nobody else (human) looking.

But, second, God's choice is conditioned on heart response. When the Bible talks of 'the heart' it means our spiritual centre, and David was God-centred. You have only to read the Psalms to see that.

> You have searched me, LORD,
>> and you know me …
>> you perceive my thoughts from afar …
> Before a word is on my tongue
>> you, LORD, know it completely …
> Search me, God, and know my heart;
>> test me and know my anxious thoughts.
> See if there is any offensive way in me,
>> and lead me in the way everlasting
>
> (Ps. 139:1, 2, 4, 23–24).

Are we like this? Are we people with a heart for God? Do we seek out such people as our close friends, our Christian leaders, our wife or husband? And what is the heart response that God looks for in each of us? We find it not only in David's psalms, but also in Solomon's proverbs, in our Lord's beatitudes (Matt. 5:3–12) and in the Spirit's fruit of which the Apostle Paul writes in Galatians 5:22–23. Indeed, Samuel should have known what God was looking for. He had just asked King Saul at the end of the preceding chapter, 'Does the LORD delight in burnt offerings and sacrifices as much as in obeying the LORD?' And Samuel continued: 'To obey is better than sacrifice' (1 Sam. 15:22). Let our prayer be that of Charles Wesley:

> O for a heart to praise my God,
> A heart from sin set free,
> A heart that always feels Thy blood
> So freely shed for me.
>
> A heart in every thought renewed,
> And full of love divine,
> Perfect and right and pure and good,
> A copy, Lord, of Thine.[2]

FOR FURTHER READING: 1 SAMUEL 16:1–13

Reflect on these points

1. *Our lives are full of choices. Will those choices be governed by the sight of our eyes or by the thoughts of God's heart?*

2. *God is more concerned with character than with*

reputation. And what is character? It's what God knows we are when we know there's nobody else (human) looking.

3. *Are we God-centred? Are we people with a heart for God? Do we seek out such people as our close friends, our Christian leaders, our wife or husband?*

God's watchful eye

At that time Tattenai ... and Shethar-Bozenai and their associates went to them [the Jews] and asked, 'Who authorised you to rebuild this temple and to finish it?' ... But the eye of their God was watching over the elders of the Jews.

(Ezra 5:3–5)

Because of their persistent idolatry and their ignoring of his word, God had allowed Israel (722 BC) and Judah (587 BC) to be taken into exile by the Babylonians. Eventually the city walls of Jerusalem, and even the temple that Solomon had built, were reduced to rubble. But around fifty years after Judah's exile, there was a major change in the fortunes of the Jewish people with the accession of the Persian king Cyrus. The first six chapters of Ezra cover a period of just over twenty years (538–515 BC) during which time a number of Jews returned from exile in Babylon with their main aim being the rebuilding of the temple. First, they had to do the fundraising (Ezra 2:68–69). Then they rebuilt the altar and restored the sacrificial system (3:2), followed by re-laying the temple foundations (3:8–13). And as the work took shape, they gave praise to God, as recorded in Ezra 3:11:

> With praise and thanksgiving they sang to the LORD:
> 'He is good;
>> his love to Israel endures for ever.'

But whenever the Lord's work prospers, so does opposition. Indeed, one could almost say that where there is no opposition, there may be little real gospel work in progress. Our Lord Jesus stated as much in John 15:18–19:

> If the world hates you, keep in mind that it hated me first. If you belonged to the world, it would love you as its own. As it is, you do not belong to the world, but I have chosen you out of the world. That is why the world hates you.

Henry Blunt (1794–1843), a leading evangelical cleric in the early nineteenth century, had this as his motto: 'I hope when things are hostile; I fear when they are favourable.'[1] What a commendable thought for any true minister of the Word!

Initially, the opponents tried to muscle in on the work as fake supporters, offering to help with the building 'because, like you, we seek your God and have been sacrificing to him since the time of Esarhaddon king of Assyria, who brought us here' (Ezra 4:2). Unbelievers in the church are nothing new, not even unbelievers who want to help run the church. But notice two clues here. To these fake supporters, God was referred to only as '*your* God' not 'our God'. They spoke more truthfully than they realized. They thought that faith could come by mere association. We often talk of 'guilt by association'. I suppose these folk believed in justification by association—that by merely hanging around God's people, they somehow would *become* God's people.

But notice also that theirs was a theology of works based on *doing* the right religious things. Sadly, many today make the same mistake, believing that by *doing* the right religious things—by being baptized, taking Communion, becoming a church member, or even by daily Bible reading—they will be put right with God. No! Not that these things in themselves are wrong—of course not; quite the contrary. But they are the *signs* and *fruits* of our having been justified, not the *cause* of it. The Apostle Paul could not have put it more clearly in Ephesians 2:8–9:

> For it is *by grace* you have been saved, through faith—
> and this is *not from yourselves*, it is *the gift of God*—
> *not by works*, so that no one can boast.

By grace, not by works; not from ourselves, but a gift from God.

The Jewish leaders declined the offer of help. It was the right decision, but hardly politically correct. Today they would doubtless be accused of exclusivity and cultural insensitivity, and would probably be referred to the equality police. What actually happened (Ezra 4:6–24) was a letter-writing campaign by the would-be helpers to the Persian authorities in an attempt to get the building work stopped. Their success is recorded at the end of the fourth chapter: the work stopped—for sixteen years. But then, at the opening of chapter 5, Haggai and Zechariah encourage the builders to restart, and, as Tiberius Rata points out, 'it is the Word of the LORD that jumpstarts the process anew'.[2] But the opposition wouldn't let it drop and turned up at the building site and asked, 'Who authorised you to rebuild this temple and to finish it?' Ominously, they even demanded the builders' names (5:4). And then comes our text: '*But* the eye of their *God* was watching over the elders of the

Jews' (5:5). When something is under the eye of God, it means it is under his watchful protection. As David writes, 'The eyes of the LORD are on the righteous, and his ears are attentive to their cry' (Ps. 34:15), words that are quoted by Peter in his first epistle (see 1 Peter 3:10–12). What a reassuring promise of the fact that God is all-seeing! As Isaac Watts (1674–1748) wrote,

> Our help is in the Lord's great name,
> The maker of the earth and sky:
> He that upholds that mighty frame
> Will guard His own with watchful eye.[3]

FOR FURTHER READING: EZRA 5:1–5

Reflect on these points

1. *Whenever the Lord's work prospers, so does opposition. Indeed, one could almost say that where there is no opposition, there may be little real gospel work in progress.*

2. *Many today make the mistake of believing that by doing the right religious things they will be put right with God. No! These things are the* signs *and* fruits *of our having been justified, not the* cause *of it.*

3. *When something is under the eye of God, it means it is under his watchful protection.*

A question of
life or death

He struck down all the firstborn of Egypt ...
But [God] *brought his people out like a flock.*

(Ps. 78:51–52)

The American car manufacturer Henry Ford (1863–1947) is reputed to have remarked that 'history is bunk'. (What he actually said was that 'history is more or less bunk'.) Well, Ford may have been right about the colour range of his Model T cars—'any colour, so long as it's black'—but he was dead wrong about history, no 'more or less' about it. His contemporary, the Spanish-born philosopher George Santayana (1863–1952), was much more on the button when he wrote that 'those who cannot remember the past are condemned to repeat it'. And that's why the Bible contains so much history, and why God has been the best and most devoted history teacher. Psalm 78 is the voice of history—God's history of God's people in God's voice. It recounts the history of the people of Israel, focusing on their deliverance from Egypt and the desert wanderings (vv. 12–53), their arrival in the Promised Land (vv. 54–55) and their chequered history in that place (vv. 56–72). The psalm contains lessons as to who God is, what he has done, how his people responded to him wrongly in the past and how they should learn from these past failures today. And why does God do all this? Verses 7 and 8 hold the answer:

> Then they would put their trust in God
>   and would not forget his deeds
>   but would keep his commands.

> They would not be like their ancestors—
>> a stubborn and rebellious generation,
> whose hearts were not loyal to God,
>> whose spirits were not faithful to him.

As we read the seventy-two verses of this psalm, we quickly discover the fickle and ungrateful nature of Israel towards their all-providing and faithful God. God blesses them. They sin. God punishes them. They repent. God blesses them again. They sin again ... You get the idea. As the psalmist writes in verses 34–41:

> Whenever God slew them, they would seek him;
>> they eagerly turned to him again.
> They remembered that God was their Rock,
>> that God Most High was their Redeemer.
> But then they would flatter him with their mouths,
>> lying to him with their tongues ...
> Yet he was merciful;
>> he forgave their iniquities
>> and did not destroy them ...
> Again and again they put God to the test;
>> they vexed the Holy One of Israel.

But are we any different? How often do we think of God—other than when we are in some fix, often brought about as a consequence of our own sin or faithlessness? I remember a preacher in a church I used to attend in Washington DC challenging us to live the coming week having God in our conscious thoughts at least once every waking hour. 'You'll probably be shocked at how challenging that is,' he added. Sadly, he was right.

Yet, despite all this, our text shows God's undeserved mercy to a people that were so faithless, unbelieving and ungrateful. The psalmist mentions seven of the first nine plagues that God visited on Egypt (vv. 44–48) and then writes that God 'struck down all the firstborn of Egypt, the firstfruits of manhood in the tents of Ham' (v. 51)—the Egyptians being the descendants of Noah's second son, Ham (Gen. 10). The awful events of that night in the Egyptian households are told in Exodus 12:29–36. Verse 30 of that chapter records that 'there was loud wailing in Egypt, for there was not a house without someone dead'.

The Egyptian firstborn were dead—'*but [God]* brought his people out' (Ps. 78:52). And how had he delivered them from the destroying angel? Through the blood of the Passover lamb, sprinkled on the doorposts of the Jewish households—for God had said, 'When I see the blood, I will pass over you' (Exod. 12:13). The American preacher James Montgomery Boice (1938–2000) once observed that you could sum up the whole of the Old Testament in four words—the question asked of Abraham by Isaac as they ascended Mount Moriah to make a sacrifice to God: 'Where is the lamb?' (Gen. 22:7). Equally, remarked Dr Boice, you can sum up the New Testament in these five words spoken by John the Baptist when he saw Jesus come towards him: 'Behold the Lamb of God' (John 1:29, KJV). Like the Jewish people back in Exodus 12, and recalled by Asaph here in Psalm 78, we too are saved by 'the blood of the Lamb'. For, as the Apostle John writes, 'If we walk in the light, as he is in the light, we have fellowship with one another, and the blood of Jesus, his Son, purifies us from all sin' (1 John 1:7). Indeed, Paul makes the parallel even more clearly when he states that 'Christ, our Passover lamb, has been sacrificed' (1 Cor. 5:7).

In Scripture, Egypt is one of the types, or figures, to mean the things of this world. Hence the writer to the Hebrews tells us that, by faith, Moses 'regarded disgrace for the sake of Christ as of greater value than the treasures of Egypt' (Heb. 11:26). And so I am bound to ask you what is truly a question of life or death: 'On the day when the Son of Man is revealed' (Luke 17:30), will you be 'struck down', having lived only for the things of this world, or will you be 'brought out' by the blood of the Lamb to dwell with him in his eternal Promised Land? It is truly a question of eternal life or death.

> Not all the blood of beasts
> On Jewish altars slain
> Could give the guilty conscience peace,
> Or wash away the stain.
>
> *But Christ*, the heavenly Lamb,
> Takes all our sins away;
> A sacrifice of nobler name,
> And richer blood than they.[1]

FOR FURTHER READING: PSALM 78

Reflect on these points

1. *Are we any different from fickle, ungrateful Israel? How often do we think of God—other than when we are in some fix, often brought about as a consequence of our own sin or faithlessness?*

2. *This is truly a question of life or death: 'On the day when the Son of Man is revealed' (Luke 17:30), will you be 'struck down', having lived only for the things of this world, or will you be 'brought out' by the blood of the Lamb to dwell with him in his eternal Promised Land?*

Excuses! Excuses!

'Alas, Sovereign LORD,' *I said, 'I do not know how to speak;
I am too young.'*

But the LORD *said to me, 'Do not say, "I am too young."'*

W hilst I was serving as a housemaster in a boarding
school in Suffolk, three of my Year 13 boys failed to
return on the last bus from Ipswich from their authorized
Saturday-night leave. I guess they thought I wouldn't wait up
for them, but I did—until they crept back into the house just
after 2 o'clock on Sunday morning. Upon asking them why
they were so late, I was told, 'We were kidnapped in Ipswich
and driven round in the boot of a car for a couple of hours, and
we've only just escaped!' As excuses go, it was one of the most
fanciful—and in hindsight most amusing—I ever heard in a
lifetime of teaching. (The truth, in case you're wondering, was
that they'd been to a nightclub in the town.)

Excuses! Excuses! The Bible has not reached its seventieth
verse before mankind starts offering excuses, as Adam blames
Eve—and by implication God himself—for his fall into sin
(Gen. 3:12). Moses is full of excuses when God commissions
him to go to Pharaoh and tell him that he, Moses, will lead
the Jewish people out of Egypt. Moses first excuses himself
on account of his being a nobody (Exod. 3:11–12), then for
not knowing God's name (3:13–22), thirdly because no one
will believe him (4:1–9), then because he's not a fluent speaker
(4:10–12), and finally because other people would be much

better for the job (4:13–17). To misquote Isaiah, Moses might just as well have said to God, 'Here I am. Send ... somebody else!' And then there are the three guests in Jesus' parable of the great banquet in Luke 14:15–24. They couldn't come to the banquet because they had 'just bought a field and ... must go and see it', or they had 'just bought five yoke of oxen' and must now go and 'try them out', or they had just got married! Excuses! Excuses!

The opening verses of the book of Jeremiah tell us quite a bit about the prophet's background. He was the son of a priest—Hilkiah—and he lived in Anathoth, a village near Jerusalem. He lived through the reigns of three kings— Josiah the reformer, Jehoiakim the despot and Zedekiah the puppet—in the years right up to the deportation of the people of Judah to Babylon. As the son of a priest, Jeremiah would have expected to have served in the priesthood. But God had other plans. And 1:4–5 tells us that God's plans even predated Jeremiah's birth:

> The word of the LORD came to me, saying,
> 'Before I formed you in the womb I knew you,
>> before you were born I set you apart;
>> I appointed you as a prophet to the nations.'

But even all this is not good enough for Jeremiah, who immediately voices two excuses as to why this job is not for him. First, he lacks eloquence. This is Jeremiah as Winnie-the-Pooh telling Owl that he is 'a Bear of Very Little Brain, and long words bother me'.[1] Or, as Philip Ryken paraphrases Jeremiah's excuse:

> Ah, wait a second, Lord, about this whole prophet-to-the-nations thing, it doesn't sound like that great an idea. Prophecy is not one of my spiritual gifts. As you know, I'm getting a C in rhetoric at the synagogue.[2]

Second, Jeremiah excuses himself on the grounds of lack of experience. 'After all, Lord, I'm only a teenager.' It's all very Moses. And then comes Jeremiah's 'but God' moment.

> *But the* LORD said to me, 'Do not say, "I am too young." You must go to everyone I send you to and say whatever I command you. Do not be afraid of them, for I am with you and will rescue you,' declares the LORD.

'Don't give me that stuff,' says God. 'You don't need to worry about your poor foreign-language skills—that maybe you're not all that fluent in Akkadian or Ugaritic.' And in the verses that follow, the Lord reaches out his hand and touches Jeremiah's mouth and says, 'Now I have put my words in your mouth.' You're ready. You're equipped. Now trust me. It's not that our gifts and skills don't matter, but Jeremiah had forgotten—and so often do we—that when it comes to work in his service, God is not limited by human weakness. Indeed, as Philip Ryken concludes, 'Enabling weak tools to do strong jobs is God's standard operating procedure', and God promises to equip those he calls. So our cry should not be

'Excuses! Excuses!' but 'Promises! Promises!' Let us pray in the words of Bishop Frank Houghton (1894–1972),

> O Father, who sustained them,
> O Spirit, who inspired,
> Saviour, whose love constrained them
> To toil with zeal untired,
> From cowardice defend us,
> From lethargy awake!
> Forth on Thy errands send us
> To labour for Thy sake.[3]

FOR FURTHER READING: JEREMIAH 1:1–10, 17–19

Reflect on these points

1. *It's not that our gifts and skills don't matter, but Jeremiah had forgotten—and so often do we—that when it comes to work in his service, God is not limited by human weakness.*

2. *God promises to equip those he calls.*

A wind, a 'whale' and a worm

But the LORD *hurled a great wind upon the sea.*

(Jonah 1:4, ESV)

But the LORD *provided a great fish to swallow Jonah.*

(1:17, NIV 1984)

But ... God *provided a worm.*

(4:7)

Jonah was on a downward spiral. God had told him to go east to Nineveh, near present-day Mosul in Iraq, but Jonah went '*down*' to Joppa (1:3, NKJV), and then went '*down*' into a ship bound for Tarshish (1:3, NKJV), probably in western Spain—in other words, in the opposite direction from God's instruction. And when a God-provided storm hit the ship and the crew looked for Jonah, he was nowhere to be found, for he had 'gone *down* into the lowest parts of the ship', where he 'had lain *down*, and was fast asleep' (1:5, NKJV). Down, down, down, down! It's worth noting how easily and quickly Jonah turns away from God. God says 'go' (1:2); Jonah says 'no!' And, like most of our disobedience, it all begins with ignoring God's word. One can surmise that upon arriving in Joppa and finding a ship bound for Tarshish, Jonah probably attributed this coincidence to 'the good hand of Providence'. How easily and conveniently we deceive ourselves! As William Banks puts it, 'When a person decides to run from God, Satan always provides complete transportation facilities.'[1] How we need to be on our guard against wandering—even running—from our God! The hymnwriter Robert Robinson (1735–1790) was honest when he wrote:

> Prone to wander, Lord, I feel it,
> Prone to leave the God I love.[2]

You might have thought that in the circumstances God would abandon his rebellious prophet. But the book of Jonah is a wonderful story of God's grace and sovereignty. And God is always true to his word, 'Never will I leave you; never will I forsake you' (Heb. 13:5). The author Malcolm Muggeridge (1903–1990) said of his own experience, 'I never wanted a God, nor ever felt any necessity to invent one. But I was driven to the conclusion that God wanted me.' To further quote Robinson's hymn:

> *Jesus sought me* when a stranger,
> Wandering from the fold of God;
> He, to rescue me from danger,
> Interposed His precious blood.

As Jonah sailed out of Joppa he must have thought, 'I've made it!' But God had other plans and, as our three lead texts show, God provided not one, not two, but three 'but God' moments to turn an errant prophet into a powerful evangelist. And as he so often does, God used the things of everyday life—a wind, a 'whale' and a worm.

Jonah thought he had escaped the mission to Nineveh, '*but the* LORD hurled a great wind upon the sea' (1:4, ESV). It's dramatic language; the word rendered 'hurled' here is the same word used when Saul 'hurled' his spear at David (1 Sam. 20:33). Today's military strategists talk proudly of 'surgical strikes' and 'precision bombing'. God knew all about that even in Jonah's day. And it's God's storm that makes Jonah reveal himself to the ship's crew and admit that he is the cause of it. 'Pick me up and throw me into the sea,' Jonah tells them (Jonah 1:12). I'm sure that at that moment Jonah thought he was going to die and was full of remorse and 'if only's. How often God speaks to us through the storms of life! As C. S. Lewis put it, 'God whispers in our pleasures, speaks in our conscience, but shouts in our pain.' I know that has been true in my life.

And the sailors do as Jonah instructed. *'But the* LORD provided a great fish' (1.17, NIV 1984)—God's second provision. And it's over this point that dinner-party rationalists vent their spleen on the most criticized fish ever to swim in the Mediterranean. We shall resist the temptation to turn it into a red herring, for the story of Jonah is not primarily about a great fish but about a great God—about his power, his sovereignty and his purposes. As with the storm, so with the fish: God makes a miraculous and saving provision for undeserving Jonah, a man who deserves punishment but receives grace. How like us!

We know the story. The prophet repents, the fish regurgitates, Jonah finally arrives in Nineveh and preaches, and those wicked folk repent and are pardoned by the same gracious God. But this offends Jonah's smug exclusivity.

Jonah's God is only for nice, deserving people. So the sailing prophet becomes the sulking prophet. When God provides a plant (4:6) to shelter him from the sun's heat, Jonah is happy again. But in the very next verse we read: '*But ... God* provided a worm' which kills the plant, much to Jonah's annoyance. God uses this as a parable so that Jonah—and we—'may have power, together with all the Lord's holy people, to grasp how wide and long and high and deep is the love of Christ, and to know this love that surpasses knowledge—that [we] may be filled to the measure of all the fullness of God' (Eph. 3:18–19).

> There's a wideness in God's mercy
> Like the wideness of the sea;
> There's a kindness in His justice
> Which is more than liberty ...
>
> For the love of God is broader
> Than the measure of man's mind;
> And the heart of the Eternal
> Is most wonderfully kind.[3]

FOR FURTHER READING: JONAH 1–4

Reflect on these points

1. *Most of our disobedience begins with ignoring God's word. How we need to be on our guard against wandering—even running—from our God!*

2. *God makes a miraculous and saving provision for*

undeserving Jonah, a man who deserves punishment but receives grace. How like us!

3. *The wicked folk of Nineveh repent and are pardoned by a gracious God. But this offends Jonah's smug exclusivity. Jonah's God is only for nice, deserving people. God uses the worm killing the plant as a parable for Jonah and for us.*

Godly
priorities

Another disciple said to [Jesus], 'Lord, first let me go and bury my father.' But Jesus told him, 'Follow me, and let the dead bury their dead.'

(Matt. 8:21–22)

Matthew's eighth chapter is mostly about Jesus' authority over disease, death, the elements and demons. First Jesus cleanses a leper (8:1–4). Then he heals the centurion's servant (vv. 5–13). This is followed by the healing of Peter's mother-in-law (vv. 14–17). Later in the same chapter, he calms the storm (vv. 23–27) and heals the demon-possessed man at Gadara (vv. 28–34). But in the middle of all this are two brief stories of would-be disciples—the first over-eager, the second over-reluctant. What Matthew wants us to understand is that the same Jesus who has authority over death, disease and the like, also has rightful authority over you and me.

In the two verses before us here, Jesus' answer seems at first glance overly harsh and utterly insensitive. A man comes to Jesus and seems to want to be a follower. Under similar circumstances, most Christian ministers would be thrilled and offer words of great encouragement. But this man has a problem with priorities. He rightly calls Jesus 'Lord', but then immediately lays down a proviso as to why he is not going to follow Jesus just now. 'First let me go and bury my father,' he says—implying that only then will he come and be a disciple of Jesus. It reminds me of the so-called prayer of Augustine of Hippo in his younger, hedonistic days: 'Lord, grant me chastity and purity, but not yet.' This would-be follower of Jesus calls Jesus 'Lord' but then proceeds to tell Jesus what is to be 'first' in his life, and it's all about self—'let *me* go and bury *my* father'—not about Jesus at all. This is not the Lordship of which our Saviour speaks, and Jesus makes this abundantly clear in his reply. This man thinks he can choose his own priorities, but Jesus tells him otherwise: 'Follow me, and let the dead bury their own dead.'

Some have interpreted Jesus as interrupting the man's funeral arrangements in mid-flow. But contemporary custom in Israel was that those who died were buried within hours. Had this young man's father just died, the young man would not have been in the crowd following Jesus but at home overseeing his father's burial with the necessary and customary haste. Clearly the man's father is still alive. He's not saying to Jesus, 'Just give me a few hours to bury my father, and I'll be right back to follow you.' Rather he is indicating that following Jesus will become convenient for him only after some years, once his father has died and he has seen to the burial. But following Christ and being his true disciple comes before even those God-given responsibilities of a son to his father. Jesus takes second place to no one; otherwise he is not truly 'Lord'. The time to believe on Jesus and to follow him is *now*. As the Apostle Paul writes to the Corinthians, 'Behold, *now* is the accepted time; behold, *now* is the day of salvation' (2 Cor. 6:2, KJV).

As with the would-be disciple whom Matthew introduces in

the three previous verses, we are not told how this young man responded to Jesus. We are left to finish the story for ourselves; to ask ourselves, what would *I* do—indeed, what have I done with Jesus' authority over my life? The presumption is that, like the rich young ruler (Mark 10:22), this man 'went away sad'. Jesus' requirements were too exacting. These men wanted discipleship on their terms. They wanted what Dietrich Bonhoeffer (1906–1945), the German pastor who suffered martyrdom at the hand of the Nazis, called the erroneous theology of 'cheap grace'—'grace without discipleship, grace without the cross, grace without Jesus Christ living and incarnate'. They wanted Christianity without Christ. But there is no such thing. There is, as Bonhoeffer says, only 'costly grace'—'the treasure hidden in the field; for the sake of it a man will gladly go and sell all that he has. It is the pearl of great price to buy which the merchant will sell all his goods. It is the kingly rule of Christ … the call of Jesus at which the disciple leaves his nets and follows him.'[1] As King David put it, 'I will not offer burnt offerings to the LORD my God that cost me nothing' (2 Sam. 24:24, ESV); or as John the Baptist expressed his relationship to Christ, 'He must increase, but I must decrease' (John 3:30, ESV).

> O the bitter shame and sorrow,
> That a time could ever be,
> When I let the Saviour's pity
> Plead in vain, and proudly answered,
> 'All of self, and none of Thee!'

The second verse of this hymn by the French Protestant pastor Théodore Monod (1836–1921) ends with the line 'Some of self, and some of Thee', and the third with 'Less of self, and more of Thee'. But finally:

> Higher than the highest heaven,
> Deeper than the deepest sea,
> Lord, Thy love at last hath conquered:
> Grant me now my supplication:
> 'None of self, and all of Thee!'

To say that from the heart is to have a truly godly priority.

FOR FURTHER READING: MATTHEW 8:18–22

Reflect on these points

1. *This would-be follower of Jesus called Jesus 'Lord' but then proceeded to tell Jesus what was to be 'first' in his life—and it was all about self, not about Jesus at all.*

2. *Following Christ and being his true disciple comes before even our God-given responsibilities. Jesus takes second place to no one; otherwise he is not truly 'Lord'.*

3. *Jesus' requirements were too exacting for these would-be disciples. They wanted discipleship on their terms, what Dietrich Bonhoeffer called 'cheap grace'.*

Peace in
the storm

Suddenly a furious storm came up on the lake, so that the waves swept over the boat. But Jesus *was sleeping.*

(*Matt. 8:24*)

' A text without context is a pretext'—so said a wise biblical expositor. The context for the text before us is that Jesus has been talking about costly discipleship, as we saw in our previous study. Jesus has just said to the teacher of the law and to the man who wants to first bury his father, 'Follow me.' And Matthew records that Jesus then got into a boat 'and his disciples followed him'. At this stage, the disciples probably had little idea what 'following Jesus' really meant. Four chapters earlier, we are told that at Jesus' call, Peter and Andrew 'at once ... left their nets and followed him' (4:20). Two verses later, Matthew records that 'immediately [James and John] left the boat and their father and followed' Jesus. In chapter 9, Matthew records that at Jesus' call to him to 'Follow me', he 'got up [from the tax collector's booth] and followed him' (9:9). This raises the most important question of all: Have you, upon hearing Jesus' call to leave those lesser loyalties of life, got up and followed him? The gospel stories are not written by the apostles so that we can admire or merely be amazed at Jesus. No; as John puts it, 'these are written that you may believe that Jesus is the Messiah, the Son of God, and that by believing you may have life in his name' (John 20:31).

But back in Matthew 8, what then happens is immediate

proof that those who do follow Jesus must expect to contend with trouble and difficulty, and, just as here for the disciples, much trouble that we meet comes upon us 'suddenly'. One day we think we are fit and healthy; the next we are told we have a serious and life-threatening illness. One day we are talking with a friend or loved one; the next he or she is taken from us by sudden death. One day we think we have a secure job; the next we are unemployed, and fear we are unemployable. Some of our most severe troubles are indeed 'furious' and the waves of distress seem to sweep over us, even to overwhelm us. And with the disciples we cry, 'Lord, save us!'

Some wrongly enter upon Christian discipleship thinking that this will mean the end to the storms of life. God loves me, they think, and has a wonderful plan for my life. If I faithfully serve Christ, all will go well for me. But the storms of life reveal the truth about our hearts. If we're doing what is right only because we think it will earn God's favour, or will force him to give us what we want, then, when our so-called faithfulness doesn't seem to be working for us, we'll grow resentful, bitter and angry at God. If we're obeying God merely to get something in return, then it's *that something* that really controls our hearts, not God. Our obedience to God is not really about pleasing *him*, but about trying to use God to get what *we* really want. It's about pleasing ourselves. And the truth is going to be revealed by our reaction whenever God doesn't give us what we really want. So what we need to learn is that the circumstances of our lives are *not* the measure of our relationship with God. God is more interested in our holiness than in our happiness.

As with so many of these 'but God' verses, this one depends for its effect on what comes before and what comes after the 'but'. Here in this verse, the 'before' is about a storm that was so furious that 'the waves swept over the boat' to such an extent, according to Luke (8:23), that the boat 'was being swamped' and the disciples were 'in great danger'. *'But Jesus'* … 'was sleeping'. This wasn't the sleep of Jonah (1:5)—the sleep of sullen carelessness. No, this was the sleep of what Dr John Harper (1924–2002) once described as 'divine carelessness'[1]— the complete lack of anxiety brought about solely by faithful trust in the sovereignty and love of God. Here was Jesus displaying both his utter trust in his Father's omnipotence and his genuine humanity—being so utterly wearied that he slept through such a violent storm.

To the disciples, such divine carelessness on Jesus' part looked like—well, carelessness. How like us. For how often do we wrongly presume that we are alone in the storms of life, that no one—not even God—knows what is happening to us. We too need to hear Jesus' gentle rebuke, 'You of little faith, why are you so afraid?' (Matt. 8:26). R. Kent Hughes asks, 'What kind of faith casts out fear?' And his answer is: 'A faith that believes the Scriptural revelation about the power and love of Christ.'[2] Do we believe with Abraham of old that 'the Lord will provide'? As John Newton put it:

> Though troubles assail and dangers affright,
> Though friends should all fail and foes all unite;
> Yet one thing secures us, whatever betide:
> The Scripture assures us, 'The Lord will provide.'
>
> No strength of our own or goodness we claim;
> Yet, since we have known the Saviour's great name,
> In this our strong tower for safety we hide,
> Almighty His power: 'The Lord will provide.'
>
> When life sinks apace and death is in view,
> The word of His grace shall comfort us through,
> Not fearing or doubting, with Christ on our side,
> We hope to die shouting: 'The Lord will provide.'[3]

FOR FURTHER READING: MATTHEW 8:23–27

Reflect on these points

1. *Have you, upon hearing Jesus' call to leave the lesser loyalties of life, got up and followed him? The gospel stories are written by the apostles so that 'you may believe' and 'have life in [Jesus'] name'.*

2. *Those who follow Jesus must expect to contend with trouble and difficulty, and much trouble that we meet comes upon us 'suddenly': the waves of distress seem to sweep over us, even to overwhelm us. And with the disciples we cry, 'Lord, save us!'*

3. *If we're obeying God merely to get something in return, then it's that something that really controls our hearts,*

not God. The truth will be revealed by our reaction whenever God doesn't give us what we really want.

4. *The circumstances of our lives are* not *the measure of our relationship with God. God is more interested in our holiness than in our happiness.*

From 'Mission Impossible' to 'Mission Accomplished'

Jesus looked at [the disciples] and said, 'With man this is impossible, but with God all things are possible.'

(Matt. 19:26)

The context of this comment by Jesus is that a man came up to him and asked, 'Teacher, what good thing must I do to get eternal life?' (Matt. 19:16). Often referred to as 'the rich young ruler', this man, in today's vocabulary, is certainly self-assured, an achiever and probably quite religious. In other words, he's just the kind of person that you or I might aspire to be, and he asks *the* big question. But it's quite clear that the mindset of this young man is that we get eternal life by earning it—through doing good things. And I suggest that's still a very common assumption today: that I get to heaven by virtue of what I do.

In the 1998 film *Saving Private Ryan*, an elite squad of US Army Rangers is given the task of finding and then rescuing Private James Ryan. As Captain John Miller, who has just found and saved Ryan, himself lies dying, he says to Ryan with his last breath, 'Earn this, earn it.' In other words, now go and live a life that is worthy of what I've done for you. 'Earning it' then becomes the focal point of the rest of James Ryan's life. And trying to 'earn it' is how many people spend their entire lives. Addressing the annual conference of the Catholic Association of Teachers in 2016, Sir Michael Wilshaw, the Chief Inspector of Schools in England, stated that the job of Christian teachers was 'about helping students to understand that by living a good life and living by Gospel values they would eventually come to God'.[1] Sir Michael needs to read his Bible rather more carefully.

Back in the Gospel of Matthew, Jesus responds by asking the young man a question: 'Why do you ask me about what is good? There is only One who is good.' By this response, Jesus reminds the young man that only God is good; in other words, no one else is good enough, so we will never 'earn' eternal life. Jesus wants the young man to stop comparing himself with those around him and start comparing himself with the only one whose opinion matters: Is he good in God's eyes? So Jesus then goes on to conduct two reality checks on him. He tells him to 'obey the commandments' (v. 17) and then (v. 18) lists six of the Ten Commandments. It's a surprising answer because it merely heaps fuel on the fire, and further boosts the man's inflated self-confidence. Predictably he answers that he's kept them all (v. 20). Although Matthew lets this go without comment, the claim is of course preposterous. But Jesus lets it go too. He doesn't challenge the fact that the man has just given false testimony about *not* giving false testimony. He just delivers the *coup de grâce*. We could paraphrase it like this: 'Ah, yes,' says Jesus, 'I'm so sorry. I wasn't aware of your achievements and legal perfection. But yes, there is one thing more you can do: sell everything you have and give all the money to the poor, and then come and follow me.' And the young man's response? The same man who just a moment ago had asked so confidently 'What do I still lack?' (v. 20), upon hearing Jesus' reply says, in effect, 'Well, yes, but I meant anything but *that*!'

At the very end of that film *Saving Private Ryan*, we see Ryan as an old man returning to the cemetery where the man who died rescuing him is buried. Falling to his knees at Captain Miller's grave, he says, 'Every day I think about what you said to me that day on the bridge. I've tried to live my life the best I could. I hope that was enough. I hope that at least in your eyes, I earned what you've done for me.' Then, turning to his wife kneeling beside him, he stammers: 'Tell me I've led a good life. Tell me I'm a good man.' Isn't that how we try to bargain with God? 'Tell me I've led a good life. Tell me I'm a good person.' But that isn't how God thinks, because not one of us can live a life good enough to compare with the utter perfection and holiness of Almighty God. As Jesus said, 'Only God is good.'

So the man 'went away sad', we are told, 'because he had great wealth' (v. 22). And then Jesus rams home the point in verse 23: 'It is easier for a camel to go through the eye of a needle than for someone who is rich to enter the kingdom of God.' Suggestions have been made that there was a small gate—called the Needle Gate—in Jerusalem. It's an engaging story, but there is no evidence that it ever existed. Instead, this is Jesus using hyperbole, saying that it would be easier to push a camel through the eye of a sewing needle than for a rich man to enter the kingdom of God. In other words, this really is 'Mission Impossible'. The disciples' reaction to this was to be 'greatly astonished' (v. 25), which suggests that they had some

flawed ideas about the kingdom of God that radically needed
changing. 'Who then can be saved?' they ask Jesus, who looks
at them and says, 'With man this is impossible, *but with God
all things are possible.*' Do you see where this is going? If we
can't earn heaven—and we can't—then the only way anyone
will ever be saved is if God operates entirely apart from us out
of his own mercy. In other words, our only hope is in God's
grace. Salvation is by grace alone, through faith alone. And
that's the only way to turn Mission Impossible into Mission
Accomplished.

> At the cross of Jesus I would take my place,
> Drawn by such a measure of redeeming grace.
> Fill my heart with sorrow, lift my eyes to see
> Jesus Christ my Saviour crucified for me.

> At the cross of Jesus pardon is complete,
> Love and justice mingle, truth and mercy meet.
> Let your love possess me, so that all may see
> What your death accomplished on the cross for me.[2]

FOR FURTHER READING: MATTHEW 19:16–26

Reflect on these points

1. *The mindset of this young man is that we get eternal life
   by earning it—through doing good things. That's still a
   very common assumption today: that I get to heaven by
   virtue of what I do.*

2. *Isn't this how we try to bargain with God: 'Tell me I've*

led a good life. Tell me I'm a good person.' But that isn't how God thinks, because not one of us can live a life good enough to compare with the utter perfection and holiness of Almighty God.

3. *If we can't earn heaven—and we can't—then the only way anyone will ever be saved is if God operates entirely apart from us out of his own mercy. In other words, our only hope is in God's grace.*

Jesus knows

Later they sent some of the Pharisees and Herodians to Jesus to catch him in his words ... But Jesus knew their hypocrisy.

(Mark 12:13–15)

The names of these two groups—the Pharisees and Herodians—probably don't mean much to many twenty-first-century readers, so let me try to help. Sending Pharisees and Herodians on a joint mission would today be like sending Nigel Farage on a mission with Jean-Claude Juncker.[1] Politically, the Pharisees were nationalists, whilst the Herodians colluded with the Roman occupiers. Theologically, the Pharisees were conservatives, whilst the Herodians were liberals. The only thing that brought them together was their hatred of Jesus. They began by flattering Jesus. 'Teacher, we know that you are a man of integrity. You aren't swayed by others, because you pay no attention to who they are; but you teach the way of God in accordance with the truth' (Mark 12:14). They'd doubtless honed and rehearsed their one about paying taxes for days: 'Is it right to pay the poll-tax to Caesar or not?' And maybe they thought, 'This time, we've got him! So let's butter him up first, then the fall will be even more spectacular.' Silence or evasion by Jesus would be disastrous. Indeed, they even seem to anticipate prevarication by adding to the question, 'Should we pay or shouldn't we?' (v. 15). It's rather like when opposition MPs ask rather raucous questions at Prime Minister's Question Time in the House of Commons, and they tack on to the question: 'Answer—yes or no!' If Jesus sided with Caesar, the people would brand him a traitor and desert him. If he didn't, Rome would deal with him as an insurrectionist. 'Should we pay or shouldn't we?' they ask shrilly. You can almost hear the smirks. Wait for it, my friends, we've got him.

But then comes the second half of verse 15: '*But Jesus* knew ...' Yes, Jesus always knows. And it wasn't just the answer to the question that he knew—though he knew that as well, of course, an answer that is astonishing both in its simplicity and profundity: 'Give back to Caesar what is Caesar's, and to God what is God's' (v. 17). But Jesus knows what is in our thoughts and even the intentions of our hearts—better than we know them ourselves. 'But Jesus knew.' Indeed, we can trace this throughout the Gospels. John records, at the very beginning of Jesus' earthly ministry, Philip bringing Nathanael to Jesus.

> When Jesus saw Nathanael approaching, he said of him, 'Here truly is an Israelite in whom there is no deceit.'
>
> 'How do *you know* me?' Nathanael asked.
>
> Jesus answered, 'I saw you while you were still under the fig-tree before Philip called you.'
>
> (John 1:47–48)

Nathanael was so struck by what Jesus knew that he replied, 'Rabbi, you are the Son of God; you are the king of Israel' (1:49).

Luke records three times in his Gospel that Jesus knew what the Pharisees were thinking before they had even said anything. After they had watched Jesus heal the paralytic, Luke says '*Jesus knew* what they were thinking' (Luke 5:22).

And when Jesus healed a demoniac, Luke records that '*Jesus knew* their thoughts', referring again to the Pharisees (11:17). John records that, when Jesus first purified the temple and many believed in him, 'Jesus would not entrust himself to them, for *he knew* all people. He did not need any testimony about mankind, for *he knew* what was in each person' (John 2:24–25). John repeatedly reminds us through his Gospel that Jesus knew what was to befall him. He knew the Father's plan and his Father's will. '*Jesus knew* that the hour had come for him to leave this world and go to the Father' (John 13:1). '*Jesus, knowing* all that was going to happen to him', confronted the soldiers who had come to arrest him (18:4). John records that at the cross, '*knowing* that everything had now been finished …, *Jesus* said, "I am thirsty"' (19:28).

What should our response be to the fact that God is all-knowing? First, we should be challenged, humbled and awed. David puts it best in Psalm 139:

> You have searched me, LORD,
>   and *you know* me.
> *You know* when I sit and when I rise;
>   *you perceive* my thoughts from afar.
> *You discern* my going out and my lying down;
>   *you are familiar with* all my ways.
> Before a word is on my tongue,
>   *you, LORD, know it completely* …
> Such knowledge is too wonderful for me,
>   too lofty for me to attain (Ps. 139:1–6).

But we should also be comforted and assured. As we dwell upon the fact that God is all-knowing (his omniscience), we are reminded also of his all-powerfulness (omnipotence) and the fact that he is all-seeing (omnipresence). We are reminded again of the time when the angel of the Lord—whom many believe to have been the pre-incarnate manifestation of Jesus—visited Hagar and told her that she would give birth to a son. And the inspired writer tells us that 'she gave this name to the LORD who spoke to her: "You are the God who sees me"' (Gen. 16:13). God still knows, and sees, and cares. As the Apostle Paul assures us, '*The* LORD *knows* those who are his' (2 Tim. 2:19).

> Have we trials and temptations?
> Is there trouble anywhere?
> We should never be discouraged;
> Take it to the Lord in prayer.
> Can we find a friend so faithful
> Who will all our sorrows share?
> *Jesus knows* our every weakness;
> Take it to the Lord in prayer.[2]

FOR FURTHER READING: MARK 12:13–17; PSALM 139

Reflect on these points

  1. *Jesus knows what is in our thoughts and even the intentions of our hearts—better than we know them ourselves.*

2. *The fact that God is all-knowing should challenge, humble and awe us.*

3. *The fact that God is all-knowing should also comfort and assure us. God still knows, and sees, and cares.*

A healing faith

Peter said, 'Master, the people are crowding and pressing
against you.'

But Jesus *said, 'Someone touched me.'*

(Luke 8:45–46)

In the second half of his eighth chapter, Luke gives us an
insight into the typical life of the Saviour. First, Jesus sails
across the Sea of Galilee and performs two miracles—one
whilst in the boat (vv. 22–25) and another immediately upon
arriving at the far shore (vv. 26–39). Then, having returned
across the water (v. 40), Jesus is met by a large, jostling crowd.
But before he can address them, he is called away to perform
another miracle—this one at the request of Jairus, a ruler of
the synagogue (vv. 41–42a). But whilst Jesus is on the way to
perform that miracle, he is interrupted to perform yet another
(vv. 42b–48). And here Luke weaves these two miracles, and
these two people's stories, into one.

The two people—the synagogue ruler and the woman with
a discharge of blood—could hardly be more different. One is a
wealthy and influential man at the top of the social ladder; the
other, a poor and insignificant woman who is not even on the
social ladder. He is a leader in the synagogue; she, according
to the law of Moses, is not allowed to even enter the temple or
participate in public worship, because of her affliction. She is
not even allowed to touch other people lest they too become
ceremonially unclean. Jairus is recorded by name; the woman
remains anonymous. Jairus comes boldly and publicly; she

comes timidly—she even comes up *behind* Jesus (v. 44) to avoid notice, and merely touches the edge of his cloak. But they both have a desperate need that only Jesus can supply. Jairus' need is the healing of his terminally ill twelve-year-old daughter; the woman's, healing from an affliction from which she has suffered since the very year that little girl was born. By interweaving these two personal dramas, Luke wants us to see that there are no hopeless cases for Jesus. Wealth and status can no more put us outside of Jesus' power than poverty and insignificance. But in this study, I want us to focus on the woman.

Luke tells us that the woman 'had been subject to bleeding for twelve years, but no one could heal her' (v. 43). Mark adds, 'She had suffered a great deal under the care of many doctors and had spent all she had, yet instead of getting better she grew worse' (5:26). Maybe Doctor Luke did not want to make such overt criticism of his professional colleagues! Matthew tells us that as she approached Jesus from behind she said to herself, 'If I only touch his cloak, I will be healed' (9:21). The Gospel writers want us to identify with her, and we should be able to do so easily. Like her, we may have come to Christ when in great physical need. The first expression of our faith may, like hers, have been simple and uninformed—almost bordering on the superstitious. But it was real. Like this woman, we were not theologians. We had no greatly developed understanding of Christian doctrine. But, praise God, we too were accepted by him. So we need not fear being rejected by him when we truly come in faith. Fear, rather, that we let him pass without responding in faith and reaching out to him. And if we are to be truly Christ's, we each need to have a moment similar to this woman's as recorded in verse 44—'She touched the edge of his cloak.' It was a touch of faith. In most of Jesus' healing miracles it is Jesus that touches the sick person. But here, Jesus is himself touched. 'And immediately,' records Luke, 'her bleeding stopped.'

Then Jesus asked, 'Who touched me?' Here is Jesus in a throng of people so dense they 'almost crushed him' (v. 42), and he wants to know who touched him! Peter—who seems to open his mouth only to change feet—is on hand to point out the folly of the enquiry. But Jesus will not be deterred, for Luke records, '*But Jesus* said, "Someone touched me."' Why should the Saviour ask who touched him, while the crowd was pressing around? We need to see that the crowd *thronged* him, but only one *touched* him. Jesus did not consider the contact of the crowd as a touch, since faith was lacking in them. And so it is for us. We may go with the crowd to church meetings, we may attend carol services at Christmas, we may pack the church for Easter Communion, but without faith we do so in vain. We may 'throng' Jesus, but we fail to 'touch' him, and so we miss his word to us—as to this woman: 'Daughter [or son], your faith has healed you. Go in peace' (v. 48).

Like this woman, we struggle with problems that we cannot cure ourselves. She was beyond human help, and so are we. We struggle with besetting sins, with broken relationships,

with incurable disabilities, with loneliness, bereavement—
the list seems endless. Like her, we spend our money on things
that do not work, that do not bring forgiveness and lasting
peace. So where do we turn when we've tried everyone and
everything else?

> Depth of mercy! can there be
> Mercy still reserved for me?
> Can my God His wrath forbear?
> Me, the chief of sinners, spare?
>
> There for me the Saviour stands;
> Shows His wounds, and spreads His hands.
> God is love! I know, I feel;
> Jesus lives, and loves me still.
>
> If I rightly read Thy heart,
> If Thou all compassion art,
> Bow Thine ear, in mercy bow;
> Pardon and accept me now.[1]

FOR FURTHER READING: LUKE 8:40–56

Reflect on these points

1. *There are no hopeless cases for Jesus. Wealth and status*
   can no more put us outside of Jesus' power than poverty
   and insignificance.

2. *Like this woman, the first expression of our faith may*
   have been simple and uninformed—but it was real. We
   need not fear being rejected by Christ when we truly

come in faith. Fear, rather, that we let him pass without responding in faith and reaching out to him.

3. *We may go with the crowd to church meetings, we may attend carol services at Christmas, we may pack the church for Easter Communion, but without faith we do so in vain. We may 'throng' Jesus, but we fail to 'touch' him, and so we miss his word to us.*

'You fool!'

Then he said, '… Take life easy; eat, drink and be merry.'
But God *said to him, 'You fool!'*

(Luke 12:18–20)

We have already seen how many times God intervenes in the lives of his servants to protect them, to warn them, to guide them. How reassuring—for the true Christian believer. But here, God intervenes in the life of someone who is clearly not following God's plan for his life—indeed, has no time or thought for God at all. How frightening.

Immediately before Jesus told this parable, Luke tells us that someone in the crowd called out to Jesus, 'Tell my brother to divide the inheritance with me' (12:13). There are doubtless still folk today who respond to the teachings of Jesus in similarly inappropriate ways. Jesus has been dealing with such crucial matters as the devil, life and death, forgiveness, blasphemy against the Holy Spirit and religious persecution, and this man's response is, 'I need more money.' Doubtless this man would have agreed with the American Zig Ziglar, who once commented that 'money isn't the most important thing in life, but it's reasonably close to oxygen on the got-to-have-it scale!'

In verses 17–19, the rich man has a 'conversation' with himself, one that is overbearingly self-centred. Ten of the forty words in his conversation—with himself—are first-person words: 'I', 'my', 'myself':

What shall *I* do? *I* have no place to store *my* crops. This

> is what *I'll* do. *I* will tear down *my* barns and build
> bigger ones, and there *I* will store *my* surplus grain.
> And *I'll* say to *myself* ...

There's clearly not a thought of God in his head. They are 'my crops' in 'my barns', 'my grain'. So 'I'll do', 'I'll tear down', 'I'll build', 'I'll store' and 'I'll say to myself ... Take life easy; eat, drink and be merry'. Everything that comes before the 'but God' moment is selfish enjoyment of the pleasures of this world: eating, drinking and merriment. Not that there's anything intrinsically wrong with any of these three activities—except when they are done with no thought for God, when they are done as the be-all and end-all of one's life.

There is irony in these words '*But God* said to him'—the fact that the man who has been having a long but entirely silent conversation with himself has been overheard by the all-hearing, all-knowing God. And God offers his two-word judgement on the man: 'You fool!' Why does God pass this judgement on him? The principal reason is that he did not know God. David writes, 'The fool says in his heart, "There is no God"' (Ps. 14:1). But here, God—yes, the God he doesn't believe in— says to the fool, 'your life will be demanded from you'. There is much irony in this too, for the word 'demanded' is the terminology of the banker calling in a loan. God is in effect saying to the man, 'Your life has always belonged to me, and now I'm coming to claim it, this very night.'

This man is a fool because he has made the gift—money— more important than the Giver—God. How enticing money is! How easily we believe its lie that it can give us security, satisfaction and self-esteem! How easily it becomes our god! Yet it's always a god that fails. As Solomon tells us, 'Whoever loves money never has enough; whoever loves wealth is never satisfied with their income' (Eccles. 5:10). When the American multi-millionaire industrialist John D. Rockefeller was asked, 'How much money is enough to make you happy?', he famously replied, 'Just a little bit more.'

Finally, God asks the rich fool a question. 'Then who will get what you have prepared for yourself?' The man had clearly never considered the truths of Psalm 49:

> Do not be overawed when others grow rich,
> > when the splendour of their house increases;
> for they will take nothing with him when they die,
> > their splendour will not descend with them.

As the oft-repeated proverb has it, 'You can't take it with you.' It reminds me of the story of two mourners chatting at the funeral of a rich friend. 'How much did he leave?' asks one. 'Everything!' replies the other. Paul writes in his first letter to Timothy, 'For we brought nothing into the world, and we can take nothing out of it' (1 Tim. 6:7). And Jesus leaves the question hanging at the end of the parable. It's the unanswered—maybe the unanswerable—question. He concludes, 'This is how it will be with whoever stores up *things* for themselves but is not rich towards *God*.' The sentence says it all: 'things' before 'God'.

How foolish indeed to look to the passing and unsatisfying

idol of money rather than be 'rich towards God'! How foolish to crave the riches of money when God offers us his *grace*—God's Riches At Christ's Expense. Paul writes to the Christians at Ephesus of 'the riches of God's grace that he lavished on us' (Eph. 1:7–8), of 'the riches of his glorious inheritance' (1:18), and of 'the incomparable riches of his grace, expressed in his kindness to us in Christ Jesus' (2:7). Let our prayer be that of William Cowper:

> The dearest idol I have known,
> Whate'er that idol be,
> Help me to tear it from Thy throne,
> And worship only Thee.[1]

FOR FURTHER READING: LUKE 12:13–21

Reflect on these points

1. *This man was a fool because he made the gift— money—more important than the Giver—God.*

2. *How enticing money is! How easily we believe its lie that it can give us security, satisfaction and self-esteem! How easily it becomes our god! Yet it's always a god that fails.*

3. *How foolish to look to the passing and unsatisfying idol of money rather than be 'rich towards God'! How foolish to crave the riches of money when God offers us his* grace—*God's Riches At Christ's Expense.*

'You fool!'

The parable of the prodigal father

So he got up and went to his father.

But ... his father *saw him and was filled with compassion for him.*

(Luke 15:20)

We are taking a bit of a liberty with our 'but God' theme by including this verse from the parable widely known as that of the prodigal son. But as 'the father' in the parable is representative of God, I trust the liberty will be excused. Indeed, the focus of Jesus' parable is not either of the sons so much as the father. And as the word 'prodigal' can mean 'extravagant' or 'lavish', it is surely the father's extravagant and lavish love for both his sons that should captivate us as we read this parable—hence 'the parable of the prodigal father'.

A thief who cashed cheques he had stolen from the postal system would not usually make the front-page news of the national press. But Alfred Parkhurst did so because he was the twenty-seven-year-old son of Irving B. Parkhurst, the assistant business manager of Harvard University. When police raided Parkhurst Junior's apartment they found evidence of his prodigal lifestyle, including receipts from the Ritz and St Regis hotels in New York City, as well as illegal drugs. Asked by the judge at his trial why he had stolen the money, Parkhurst replied that it was 'because I like to have a good time'. When sentencing him to two years in prison, the judge said he could not understand how a man of his 'background and intelligence could descend to the level of a common thief'. How foolish of the judge to imagine that 'background and intelligence' can shield us from the world's enticements! He should have read this parable.

Let's first observe the context in which Jesus told it, given by Luke in the chapter's first two verses:

> Now the tax collectors and sinners were all gathering round to hear Jesus. But the Pharisees and the teachers of the law muttered, 'This man welcomes sinners and eats with them.'

These outwardly pious folk could not understand—and, what is more, were annoyed by—God's lavish mercy shown to needy sinners. The parable is one of the most remarkable Jesus ever told, but if we look at it carefully it is utterly shocking. First, the younger son's demand that his father give him his share of the inheritance (v. 12) is scandalous. The son is asking for what he will inherit once his father has died, so by demanding it now the son is really saying to his father, 'I wish you were dead!' What scandalous behaviour! But the father responds to this outrageous and hurtful request with unimaginable generosity.

We know how the story develops—the boy's journey to the 'distant country' and the squandering of his inheritance in 'wild living' (v. 13), all doubtless justified to himself as just 'liking to have a good time'. But after the feast comes the famine (v. 14), and the boy reaches rock bottom as a hired hand on a pig farm (vv. 15–16). Can you imagine anything more shocking—a Jewish man on a Gentile pig farm!

But then comes repentance and conversion, and the son

composes his own prayer (vv. 18–19) in which he will confess his sin to his father and give recognition of the fact that he is 'no longer worthy' to be called a son. In this he echoes the words of the Roman centurion who sent word to Jesus: 'Lord … I am not worthy to have you come under my roof' (Luke 7:6, ESV). This is the only way in which you and I can approach a holy God: 'Just as I am, without one plea, but that Thy blood was shed for me.' In and of ourselves we are entirely unworthy. What kind of reception did the son expect from his father upon his return? What kind of reception do we expect from God when we return as sinners? One can only imagine that the son expected anger, rebuke and withering scorn. (That is, after all, what he would indirectly receive from his older brother.) But no! Now comes our verse:

> *But* while he was still a long way off, *his father* saw him and was filled with compassion for him; he ran to his son, threw his arms round him and kissed him.

What amazing grace! What extravagant love! The implication is that each day the father had been scanning the horizon for his lost son. No one had to tell him that his son had arrived: he saw him coming. And the first emotion the father felt was compassion.

But then the prodigal father doesn't wait for his son to walk the remaining steps—he runs to meet him, and running for a Jewish gentleman was very undignified. Philip Ryken describes 'the extraordinary spectacle of a distinguished, landed gentleman hitching up his robes and racing down the street, bare legs and all'.[1] Then the father starts to kiss his errant son. Indeed, the Greek tense tells us that he kissed him again and again. There is no criticism, no inquisition, no 'how could you do such a thing to me?' And when the son begins his prepared confession (v. 21), the father cuts him off before he can get to the bit about becoming his father's hired hand, in order to summon up a new wardrobe. And then the feasting begins. As Luke recorded Jesus saying just a few verses earlier:

> There will be more joy in heaven over one sinner who repents than over ninety-nine righteous people who do not need to repent (15:7).

Have you come home to your loving heavenly Father and experienced the joy of being accepted once more by him as a true child of God?

FOR FURTHER READING: LUKE 15

Reflect on these points

1. *This is the only way in which you and I can approach a holy God: 'Just as I am, without one plea, but that Thy blood was shed for me.' In and of ourselves we are entirely unworthy.*

2. *What kind of reception do we expect from God when we return as sinners? Maybe we expect anger, rebuke and withering scorn. But no! What amazing grace! What extravagant love!*

3. *Have you come home to your loving heavenly Father*

and experienced the joy of being accepted once more by him as a true child of God?

Silence that is *not* golden

[Herod] plied him with many questions, but Jesus *gave him no answer.*

(Luke 23:9)

Fifty years ago, The Tremeloes—a pop group of four fresh-faced young lads from Dagenham in East London—were sitting atop the UK singles chart with their hit song 'Silence Is Golden'. But silence is not always golden. Indeed, silence can be quite disconcerting. I was once staying in a small hotel tucked away in a remote glen between Inverness and Fort Augustus. The only way in was up a two-mile track. I loved the silence of it all. But I remember one morning when a couple who had arrived just the previous evening told the hotelier that they would be leaving because 'it's just too quiet'. They were used to city noise and could not cope without it. To them, silence was not golden.

Our text is set early in the morning of the first Good Friday. Jesus has been arrested the previous evening, and at daybreak (Luke 22:66) appears before the Jewish Sanhedrin who, in a show trial, claim he is guilty of blasphemy and therefore deserves to die. But the Jews do not have the authority to sentence him to death, so Jesus is taken by them to Pilate (23:1). The trouble is that the Romans did not consider blasphemy a crime so the Jews have to change the charges to those of political subversion and tax avoidance (23:2)—both patently false.

The American actor and humourist Will Rogers (1879–1935)

once remarked, 'There have been two great eras in American history: the passing of the buffalo and the passing of the buck.' Pilate was a buck-passer and sent Jesus to Herod (v. 7). This was Herod Antipas who, along with his wife Herodias, had been the subject of personal criticism by John the Baptist. Herodias was the daughter of Herod's half-brother and thus his niece. Furthermore, when he met her she was married to another of his half-brothers, Herod Philip, and was therefore also his sister-in-law. Unperturbed, he seduced her and married her in an act that clearly violated Jewish law. It was this state of affairs that brought about John's denunciation of Herod Antipas—'It is not lawful for you to have your brother's wife' (Mark 6:18)—as well as Herodias' grudge against John. Mark further records in his Gospel that Herodias wanted to kill John 'but she was not able to, because Herod feared John and protected him, knowing him to be a righteous and holy man' (6:19–20). Whilst John was imprisoned by Herod on trumped-up political charges, Herod would send for him and have him preach. 'When Herod heard John,' continues Mark, 'he was greatly puzzled; yet he liked to listen to him.'

What curious behaviour! But it's possible even today to sit under the preaching of God's Word, even to 'like' it, and yet to remain totally unmoved by it. Maybe it salves our conscience. We've done our 'good deed for the day'; we've 'done church'. The danger is that after a period of time our conscience becomes anaesthetized by the gospel message. The story of how Herod was tricked by his wife into executing John is well known (Mark 6:21–29). Mark further records that when later Herod heard of Jesus' miracles he said, 'John, whom I beheaded, has been raised from the dead!' (6:16). In the Greek, the 'I' is emphatic—'I am the one: I did it!' Herod's past sins worried him. But there was no repentance.

And now he meets the Saviour he so desperately needs. But it's too late, for by now Herod has no spiritual interest in Jesus at all. He sees him only as a figure of fun, a provider of cheap entertainment. For Luke now tells us that upon hearing that Pilate was sending Jesus to him, 'he was greatly pleased, because for a long time he had been wanting to see him' because 'he hoped to see him perform a sign of some sort' (Luke 23:8). The sin-hardened Herod had become gospel-hardened too. Whatever flickers of conscience there might have been in earlier days had well and truly been snuffed out to such an extent that even meeting the Son of God could not elicit a realization of his desperate spiritual needs. Oh, what a warning! And now Herod 'plied [Jesus] with many questions, *but Jesus* gave him no answer' (v. 9).

In the vast majority of our 'but God' texts, what precedes these two words is indicative of human sinfulness and misery, and what follows speaks of God's grace and God's rescue. But not here. Herod asks questions of Jesus and is met by a stony, awful silence. And that silence is even more appalling when one considers those whom Jesus had conversed with in those hours immediately preceding his appearance before Herod. He had been prepared to answer Pilate's question (v. 3). He had answered the question put to him by Caiaphas and the Sanhedrin (22:67–69). He had even conversed with Judas at the moment of his betrayal in the Garden (22:48), reaching out tenderly to the betrayer: 'Judas, are you betraying the Son of Man with a kiss?' This was a silence that certainly was not golden.

So why did Jesus not speak to Herod? Maybe it was because Herod wouldn't have believed him anyway. Maybe it was another sign of Jesus' acceptance of his Father's will. But maybe it was because Herod's day of grace had passed and there was nothing left for Jesus to say to him. What a warning to any who reject God's grace; '*now* is the day of salvation' (2 Cor. 6:2).

> Speak, Lord, in the stillness,
> While I wait on Thee;
> Hushed my heart to listen,
> In expectancy.
>
> Speak, Thy servant heareth,
> Be not silent, Lord;
> Waits my soul upon Thee
> For the quickening word.[1]

For further reading: Luke 23:1–12

Reflect on these points

  1. *It's possible to sit under the preaching of God's Word, even to 'like' it, and yet to remain totally unmoved by it.*

The danger is that after a period of time our conscience becomes anaesthetized by the gospel message.

2. *The sin-hardened Herod had become gospel-hardened. Whatever flickers of conscience there might have been in earlier days had well and truly been snuffed out to such an extent that even meeting the Son of God could not elicit a realization of his desperate spiritual needs.*

3. *Why did Jesus not speak to Herod? Maybe it was because Herod's day of grace had passed and there was nothing left for Jesus to say to him. What a warning to any who reject God's grace!*

The unique
Christ

No one has ever seen God, but the one and only Son, who is himself God ... *has made him known.*

(John 1:18)

French Christians will be familiar with John 3:16 as '*Car Dieu a tant aimé le monde qu'il a donné son Fils unique*'. Literally this means, 'For God loved the world so much that he gave his *unique* Son.' In the Greek, the word rendered 'unique' is *monogenes*, which the New International Version translates as 'the one and only'. Hence, in John 1:14 we read that:

> The Word became flesh and made his dwelling among us. We have seen his glory, the glory of *the one and only Son*, who came from the Father, full of grace and truth.

Thus in our text, 'the one and only' is Jesus. And here, as with so many of our 'but God' texts, what precedes 'but God' contrasts sharply with what follows it. So first let us consider the start of the verse: 'no one has ever seen God.'

The Old Testament Scriptures bore witness to the invisibility of God. Moses was told by God that 'no one may see me and live' (Exod. 33:20). King Solomon told of how God dwelt in 'thick darkness' (1 Kings 8:12, ESV), and the prophet Elijah did not see God but merely heard 'a still small voice' (1 Kings 19:12, KJV). The Scottish minister William Chalmers Smith (1824–1908) was once invited to stay with a friend who lived in a beautiful part of the Scottish Highlands. He had been promised spectacular mountain views from the house. But for the whole of the time of his visit, the mountains remained shrouded by rain and low cloud, and he saw nothing of what his friend assured him would have been truly spectacular. 'How like God,' thought the cleric: spectacular, but invisible; and he penned what would become his most famous hymn:

> Immortal, invisible, God only wise,
> In light inaccessible *hid from our eyes*.

In the Old Testament, God had made partial revelations of his glory in a number of theophanies. These were visible appearances of someone who appeared to be human yet who was also in some ways divine—often referred to as 'the angel of the LORD'. One such appearance was given to Moses in the burning bush (Exod. 3:1–6). Another appeared to Ezekiel at his commissioning as a prophet (Ezek. 1). But these were revelations of the *glory* of God—not of God himself. They were partial revelations of the invisible God. But then came a fuller revelation of God to humankind—the incarnation of Jesus Christ.

Antonin Scalia (1936–2016), the one-time justice of the United States Supreme Court, once told of the time when he was about to leave Georgetown University having completed his history degree:

> I went before a panel of three professors who quizzed you. The chairman was a lovely man, a wonderful man, and he's giving me these questions. And I'm knocking them out of the ball-park, and I'm feeling

really good. Then he says, 'Very good, Mr. Scalia. I
have one last question: If you look back over all the
history that you've studied here, if you had to pick
one event that you thought was the most significant,
what would it be?'

And I'm thinking, there's no wrong answer to this.
I don't remember what I even answered, maybe the
Battle of Waterloo ... And he shook his head sadly
and said, 'No, Mr. Scalia. The Incarnation of God in
becoming man in the form of Jesus Christ.' That was
the last lesson I learned at Georgetown.[1]

Scalia had realized the significance of the 'but God'
intervention in John 1:18. Yes, God is invisible, *but the one
and only Son, who is himself God*—that is, Jesus—'has
made him known', and that is the most significant event
in all of history. In his Gospel, Matthew (1:23) tells us that
the incarnation was itself a fulfilment of prophecy (Isa.
7:14) that 'they will call him Immanuel (which means "God
with us")'. Jesus is therefore unique—uniquely qualified to
reveal God to us. 'Anyone who has seen me has seen the
Father,' Jesus told his disciples (John 14:9). The Apostle
Paul tells the Colossian Christians that Jesus 'is the [visible]
image of the invisible God' (Col. 1:15) and that 'in Christ
all the fullness of the Deity lives in bodily form' (2:9). John
Stott described the incarnation of Jesus as 'the outward
shining of the inward being of God'.[2] So today, if you want

to see God, look at Jesus. That's why Christianity without Christ is nothing.

And here is another way in which Jesus is unique: he's uniquely able to save us from sin and eternal death. That's why he claims to be the *only* way to God, saying, 'I am the way and the truth and the life. No one comes to the Father *except through me*' (John 14:6). Do you believe that Jesus is the unique Son of God, the unique Saviour, the only person through whom we can know the one true God? C. S. Lewis surveyed all the evidence and concluded:

> I am trying to prevent anyone saying the really foolish thing that people often say about him: 'I'm ready to accept Jesus as a great moral teacher, but I don't accept his claim to be God.' That is the one thing we must not say. A man who was merely a man and said the sort of things Jesus said would not be a great moral teacher. He would either be a lunatic, or else he would be the Devil of hell. You must make your choice. Either this man was, and is, the Son of God: or else a madman or something worse. But let us not come with any patronising nonsense about his being a great human teacher. He has not left that open to us. He did not intend to.[3]

We must all decide, for even to avoid a decision is itself a decision. Pontius Pilate tried that route—and publicly and literally washed his hands of Jesus. But even he decided. What have you decided?

FOR FURTHER READING: JOHN 1:1–18

Reflect on these points

1. *Jesus is unique—uniquely qualified to reveal God to us.*

2. *If you want to see God, look at Jesus. That's why Christianity without Christ is nothing.*

3. *Jesus is also uniquely able to save us from sin and eternal death. That's why he claims to be the* only *way to God.*

4. *We must all decide whether we believe this, for even to avoid a decision is itself a decision.*

I know that my Redeemer lives!

And you ... put [Jesus] to death by nailing him to the cross. But God raised him from the dead.

(Acts 2:23–24)

'*B*ut God raised him from the dead.' This key gospel truth about Jesus appears no fewer than five times in the first half of the book of Acts. It first appears here in chapter 2, where Peter is preaching his Pentecost sermon. A chapter later, Peter is preaching in Solomon's Colonnade, where he proclaims, 'You killed the author of life, *but God* raised him from the dead' (3:15). In the next chapter Peter is asked by the Sanhedrin how he has healed the crippled man. Peter replies, 'It is by the name of Jesus Christ of Nazareth, whom you crucified *but whom God* raised from the dead' (4:10). Then in chapter 10, Peter is preaching in the house of Cornelius and states, 'They [the Jews] killed him [Jesus] by hanging him on a cross, *but God* raised him from the dead' (10:39–40). Finally in chapter 13 Paul, preaching in Antioch in Pisidia, proclaims, 'When they [the Jews] had carried out all that was written about him [Jesus], they took him down from the cross and laid him in a tomb. *But God* raised him from the dead' (13:29–30). Any good teacher will tell you that repetition is an excellent teaching technique. So when the Bible tells us something *five* times in just twelve chapters, you can be sure it's of the utmost importance.

Furthermore, what we are studying here is the first Christian sermon and it contains within it the paradox that the death of Jesus was both the result of human wickedness and the foreordained purpose of God. Peter begins by attesting to the historical Jesus—the man who only weeks before had displayed 'miracles, wonders and signs, which God did among you through him, as you yourselves know' (2:22). But the death of Jesus was no accident, as verse 23 explains. First, there were the 'fellow Israelites' (v. 22) who were responsible, 'with the help of wicked men' (v. 22)—clearly a reference to the Roman authorities in the guise of Herod and Pontius Pilate. It was a shared responsibility. Indeed, Jesus himself had made the culpability of mankind as a whole very clear in the parable of the vineyard owner in Mark 12.

But, second, we must see God's purposes and plan. For verse 22 tells us that Jesus 'was handed over to you by God's deliberate plan and foreknowledge'. Throughout his Gospel, Luke, the author of Acts, stressed the sovereign overruling of God in the death of Jesus. Remember Luke's account of the disciples on the Emmaus road and Jesus' post-resurrection teaching: 'Did not the Messiah have to suffer these things ... And beginning with Moses and all the Prophets, he explained to them what was said in all the Scriptures concerning himself' (Luke 24:26–27).

But we need to go further. For Peter says to the Pentecost crowds, 'You ... put him to death', and it is important that we see the true significance of that statement for us today. For as the Good Friday hymn clearly states:

> We may not know, we cannot tell,
> What pains He had to bear,

> But we believe it was *for us*
> He hung and suffered there.[1]

Yes, 'for us'—for you and for me. Do you truly believe that? The great Dutch painter Rembrandt (1606–1669) portrayed Christ's crucifixion more than once. But in one of those paintings, he portrayed all the characters one might expect— Jesus, the two thieves, the crowd, the women—and also, down in a corner, Rembrandt placed his own face in the crowd, as if to say, 'I was there too. I witnessed, I caused, his death.'

> Behold the man upon a cross,
> *My* sin upon His shoulders;
> Ashamed, I hear *my* mocking voice
> Call out among the scoffers.
> It was *my* sin that held Him there
> Until it was accomplished …[2]

As so often in these 'but God' verses, everything that immediately precedes expresses some of the worst of human atrocities and stark examples of human disobedience and rebellion against God. What could be worse than killing the spotless Lamb of God? Before the phrase 'but God', all is hopeless, dark and heading for everlasting death. But after 'but God' we find God's glorious and undeserved grace, mercy and love. Indeed, the cross of Christ can be seen as the greatest 'but God' moment of human history. '*But God* raised him from the dead!' Oh, what a glorious truth! And so I ask again, do you truly believe it? Can you say with Job of old, 'I *know* that my

149

redeemer lives' (Job 19:25)? As Paul reminds the Corinthians, 'If Christ has not been raised, your faith is futile; you are still in your sins' (1 Cor. 15:17). Here is the very key to the Christian gospel.

> I know that my Redeemer lives;
> O the sweet joy this sentence gives!
> He lives, He lives, who once was dead;
> He lives, my everlasting Head![3]

Alleluia!

FOR FURTHER READING: ACTS 2:22–39

Reflect on these points

1. '... *It was* for us *He hung and suffered there'—for you and for me. Do you truly believe that?*

2. *The cross of Christ can be seen as the greatest 'but God' moment of human history. 'But God raised him from the dead!' Oh, what a glorious truth!*

3. *Can you say with Job of old, 'I know that my redeemer lives' (Job 19:25)?*

I know that my Redeemer lives!

How do I know God loves me?

Very rarely will anyone else die for a righteous person ... But God demonstrates his own love for us in this: while we were still sinners, Christ died for us.

(Rom. 5:7–8)

During the American Revolutionary War there was a faithful preacher of the gospel by the name of Peter Miller. Living near him was a man who hated him intensely because of Miller's Christian life and testimony. One day Miller's neighbour was found guilty of treason and sentenced to death. Hearing of this, Miller interceded for the man's life before George Washington. Washington listened but told him he didn't feel he could pardon his friend. 'He's not my friend,' said Miller. 'In fact, he's my worst living enemy.' Upon learning that Miller had walked sixty miles to save the life of his enemy, Washington decided to pardon the man. So, with pardon in hand, Miller arrived at the place of execution just as the prisoner was walking to the scaffold. When the man saw Miller arrive he exclaimed, 'Old Peter Miller has come to have his revenge by watching me hang!' But he was utterly astonished as he watched the minister step out of the crowd, produce the pardon and save his life.

What Peter Miller did was indeed a noble act, but it is only a poor and pale shadow of what Christ has done for you and for me, because Christ not only obtained the pardon, but he died a cruel and brutal death on the cross in order to accomplish that. True, many have died so that others could live. But Jesus did not die in order to extend our lives by a few years, or even a few decades. Rather, he died to extend our lives for ever—for eternity.

In these and the surrounding verses in Romans 5, Paul has some astounding things to say about how Christ won our salvation. First, Paul tells us that the timing was of God's choosing: 'At just the right time,' Paul says in verse 6, 'when we were still powerless, Christ died for the ungodly.' It was the fulfilment of God's perfect plan, in God's perfect time. The Apostle John records in his Gospel that when the Jews in Judea 'were looking for a way to kill' Jesus (John 7:1), Jesus purposely stayed away, telling his disciples that 'my time is not yet here' (7:6).

Second, Paul reminds us that God did not wait for us to become righteous—or even deserving—before he brought about our redemption. He did it 'when we were still powerless' and in a state of ungodliness (Rom. 5:6).

Third, in verse 7, Paul points out that even 'righteous' or 'good' people would find it hard to get someone to die for them—even though they might be thought of as deserving, or through their goodness might have generated some sort of affection or devotion. But the whole point, of course, is that Jesus did not die for people who were either righteous or good. You have only to read Paul's argument in the opening chapter of Romans to see how fallen humankind is not exactly kindly disposed towards God:

> For although they knew God, they neither glorified him as God nor gave thanks to him, but their thinking became futile and their foolish hearts were darkened ...

Furthermore, just as they did not think it worth while to retain the knowledge of God, so God gave them over to a depraved mind, so that they do what ought not to be done. They have become filled with every kind of wickedness, evil, greed and depravity. They are full of envy, murder, strife, deceit and malice. They are gossips, slanderers, God-haters, insolent, arrogant and boastful; they invent ways of doing evil; they disobey their parents; they have no understanding, no fidelity, no love, no mercy. Although they know God's righteous decree that those who do such things deserve death, they not only continue to do these very things but also approve of those who practise them (Rom. 1:21, 28–32).

But God! '*But God* demonstrates his own love for us in this: while we were still sinners, Christ died for us.' As R. C. Sproul puts it, 'While we were being actively disobedient to God, while we were in a state of rebellion against God, while we were hostile to God, while we were ignoring God, while we were refusing to submit to him, refusing to love him, refusing to worship him, at that time, while we were at enmity with God, Christ died for us.'[1]

You may know the story of the Swiss theologian Karl Barth (1886–1968) who was asked at the end of one of his lectures, 'Dr Barth, what is the greatest thought that has ever gone through your mind?' The questioner probably expected some complicated and incomprehensible answer. But after a long pause, Barth replied, 'Jesus loves me, this I know, for the Bible tells me so.' This is truly a simple and yet profound answer.

In March 2002, I was recuperating in Suffolk after an operation for cancer and spent Good Friday afternoon in the cathedral at Bury St Edmunds. The sermons during the three-hour service that day were preached by Professor Hugh Williamson, then Regius Professor of Hebrew at the University of Oxford. One line from his sermons which spoke so clearly to me that afternoon was this challenge: 'So how do I know the love of God? Because when I prayed he gave me that good job? No! Because when I prayed he cured that illness? No! But because he sent his only begotten Son to die for my sin.' That's how I know God loves me.

> It is a thing most wonderful,
> Almost too wonderful to be,
> That God's own Son should come from heaven,
> And die to save a child like me.
>
> And yet I know that it is true:
> He chose a poor and humble lot,
> And wept and toiled, and mourned and died,
> For love of those who loved Him not.[2]

FOR FURTHER READING: ROMANS 5:1–8

Reflect on these points

1. *Christ not only obtained the pardon, but he died a cruel*

and brutal death on the cross in order to accomplish that.

2. *Jesus did not die in order to extend our lives by a few years, or even a few decades. Rather, he died to extend our lives for ever—for eternity.*

3. *Jesus did not die for people who were either righteous or good: 'while we were still sinners, Christ died for us.'*

4. *'How do I know the love of God? … Because he sent his only begotten Son to die for my sin.'*

Sin's wages ...
God's gift

For the wages of sin is death, but the gift of God *is eternal life in Christ Jesus our Lord.*

(Rom. 6:23)

Have you ever written a thank-you note to your employer for the wages or salary you had just received? Or how many of us, upon receiving a birthday or Christmas gift from a family member or friend, would ask that person the cost of the gift and then hand over the money to cover the cost? Both scenarios are bizarre. We know the difference between wages (that are earned) and gifts (that are freely given) in everyday life. Well, it's equally important to know the difference between a wage and a gift in our spiritual lives.

Like so many of our 'but God' texts, it is what comes before these two words that gives this text its power. It is often when things are very bad—indeed, humanly beyond redemption (sometimes literally)—that God steps in and effects the critical life-saving difference. Furthermore, this verse contains three important contrasts: a gift as against a wage; God as against sin; eternal life as against death.

But what is sin? Sin is transgression of God's law. It is failure to reach moral perfection; failure to treat either God or our fellow human beings as we ought. It was against this understanding that Paul concluded three chapters earlier that '*all* have sinned and fall short of the glory of God' (Rom. 3:23).

The immediate context of our text is Paul's question posed in verse 15: 'What then? Shall we sin because we are not under the law but under grace?'—to which the apostle gives his emphatic answer, 'By no means!' Paul then uses the image of the master and the slave to make the point that we're all slaves to someone or something. 'You are slaves of the one you obey,' says Paul (v. 16), 'whether you are slaves to sin, which leads to death, or to obedience, which leads to righteousness.' Mention of slavery would certainly have got the attention of Paul's readers. Some would have been freed slaves whilst others would still have been slaves. So the truth of verse 16 would have been easily understood.

What is more, as the Roman church assembled to hear Paul's letter, it would not have been obvious who amongst the congregation were slaves and who were not. One might have unknowingly been sitting next to a slave. And the same is true in today's church. Of course, the types of enslavement today are different from those in Paul's day, but they are no less enslaving. Some will be enslaved to their work, others to leisure; some will be enslaved to their possessions, others to their families, their sports, their physical bodies, their tempers, their sexual desires—the list of possibilities is endless. Far more deeply, many will still be in slavery to sin—yes, even in church. In this sense, nothing has changed from New Testament times. The Apostle John records an exchange between Jesus and the Pharisees—the most pious and religious folk of his day. Jesus was speaking to them about the gospel and said,

> If you hold to my teaching, you are really my disciples.

Then you will know the truth, and the truth will set you free (John 8:31–32).

But the Pharisees were having none of it. 'We are Abraham's descendants,' they replied indignantly. In today's parlance, we could substitute, 'we are Church of England', 'we are evangelicals', or 'we've been baptized'. And so the Pharisees continued, '[We] have never been slaves of anyone. How can you say that we shall be set free?' (8:33). But Jesus replied to them, as he does to us: 'Very truly I tell you, everyone who sins is a slave to sin' (8:34). And according to our text, the wages that sin pays to its slaves is death—not just physical death, but eternal death, eternal separation from God.

However, in stark contrast to sin's *wages* of death, God's *gift* is 'eternal life in Christ Jesus our Lord'. God's gift to us is salvation and, like all other gifts, God's gift is free: he alone does the giving, and our part is played only in the receiving. But so often we like to imagine that we can *earn* our salvation—by churchgoing, or leading a 'good life'. But one cannot earn a gift.

When men go to get their hair cut, the conversation between the barber and the customer often focuses on sport, politics or religion. There's a story about a Christian man who was having his hair cut and the conversation had got on to the Christian gospel, with the customer explaining how on the cross Jesus had accomplished everything necessary for our salvation. But the barber was having none of it.

'That can't be right,' he told the customer. 'I have to *do* things to get right with God. I have to go to church every Sunday.'

'No you don't,' the customer replied. 'Going to church doesn't make you right with God. Jesus has done all that, on the cross. It's done. It's finished.'

But the barber protested, 'No, I have to lead a good life.'

'No,' insisted the customer, 'it's all finished, it's all done.'

'No, that just can't be right,' said the barber again as he finished cutting the man's hair and held up the mirror for the customer to admire his handiwork.

Suddenly the customer grabbed the scissors from the barber and began hacking at his hair. 'No, stop!' the barber shouted. 'It's finished, it's done.'

'Yes, precisely!' said the customer. 'It's finished, it's done!'

When Jesus died on the cross to pay the penalty for your sin, he said 'It is *finished!*' It's done. So there's nothing more for you to do other than accept by faith that Jesus has died for your sin, paid the penalty for you, and that thereby you can be right with God—and enjoy eternal life.

> Not what these hands have done
> Can save this guilty soul;
> Not what this toiling flesh has borne
> Can make my spirit whole.
>
> *Thy* grace alone, O God,
> To me can pardon speak;
> *Thy* power alone, O Son of God,
> Can this sore bondage break.[1]

FOR FURTHER READING: ROMANS 6:15–23

Reflect on these points

1. *The types of enslavement are different from in Paul's day, but they are no less enslaving. And the wages that sin pays to its slaves is death—eternal death, eternal separation from God.*

2. *God's gift is free: he alone does the giving, and our part is played only in the receiving. So often we like to imagine that we can* earn *our salvation. But one cannot earn a gift.*

3. *When Jesus died on the cross to pay the penalty for your sin, he said 'It is* finished!' *So there's nothing more for you to do other than accept by faith that Jesus has died for your sin, paid the penalty for you, and that thereby you can be right with God—and enjoy eternal life.*

The burden-bearer

We do not know what we ought to pray for, but the Spirit *himself intercedes for us ...*

(Rom. 8:26)

We have looked at a number of Scripture verses containing the phrase 'but God ...' and others with the phrase 'but Jesus ...' Here in the eighth chapter of Romans, Paul writes *'but the Spirit ...'*, thereby introducing the third person of the Trinity to our selected verses. We learn much of Jesus' teaching about the Holy Spirit in John 14, where he tells the apostles, 'If you love me, keep my commands. And I will ask the Father, and he will give you another advocate to help you and be with you for ever—the Spirit of truth' (John 14:15–17). The Greek word translated 'advocate' (or 'Counsellor', 'Helper' or 'Comforter' in other translations) is *paraklētos,* literally 'someone called alongside to help'. And Jesus promised 'another' someone-called-alongside-to-help. There are two ways one can use the word 'another'. If you buy an item from a store only to discover when you get home that it doesn't work, you return to the store and ask for *'another'* one. Clearly you mean another one but *different*—one that works. On the other hand, you could buy a child an ice cream, which he adores. He eats it quickly and then asks, 'May I have *another* one?'—in other words, one exactly the same as I've just had. It's the latter meaning we have in John 14:16: the Father, says Jesus, will give you another—exactly the same as you've just had—advocate. In other words, Jesus is telling us that the Holy Spirit is exactly the same as him, which is why we should always refer to the Holy Spirit as 'he' and not 'it'. He's a person, not a power.

Back in Romans 8, Paul writes, 'In the same way, the Spirit helps us in our weaknesses' (8:26). 'In the same way' as what? Martyn Lloyd-Jones, in his commentary on Romans, suggests that Paul is here referring back to verses 15–17, where Paul teaches that the Holy Spirit enables us to pray as God's adopted children, addressing God as 'Abba, Father'. Now, says Paul, 'in the same way, the Spirit helps us in our weakness'—our weakness in prayer; for, continues the apostle, 'we do not know what we ought to pray for'. Do you, like me, find prayer a problem? And maybe you also *worry* that you find prayer a problem. Does it suggest that you are not really spiritual? Well, if we have never come to God in true repentance and faith, then we would not be his adopted children and would have no right to call God 'Father', nor would we have the Holy Spirit to help us to pray. But the Bible is full of promises that whoever comes to God claiming the forgiveness that Christ won on the cross will be, as the hymn puts it, 'ransomed, healed, restored, forgiven'.[1]

But what about those of us who *are* God's children? We should be reassured that the Bible tells us of truly godly people who struggled with not knowing what they should pray for. Job and Elijah are two such examples. And notice, too, that Paul includes himself in this problem, for he writes of '*our* weakness'. This weakness may come in a number of guises.

It may be physical weakness—we are just in so much pain, or simply so weary, that we do not know what or how to pray. It may be weakness of ignorance or a lack of understanding as to what God's will is for our lives, and so 'we do not know what we ought to pray for'. '*But the Spirit* himself intercedes for us.' We are weak, but the Spirit is all-powerful. The American Bible teacher A. T. Robertson (1863–1934) pictured it thus: 'The Holy Spirit lays hold of our weaknesses along with us and carries his part of the burden facing us, as if two men were carrying a log, one at each end.'[2] Thus the Holy Spirit becomes our burden-bearer.

But there is more, for Paul continues, 'But the Spirit himself intercedes for us through wordless groans.' This links with the idea of carrying a heavy burden, for a groan is appropriate to burden-bearing. In his exposition on this verse, James Montgomery Boice uses the illustration of two people trying to move a piano, when only one is doing the heavy lifting:

> Suppose the other is saying, 'My, that piano looks very heavy. They certainly do make pianos heavy and awkward. Probably we should have spent some money and hired professional piano movers.' If you were struggling with that heavy load, that is probably the last thing you want to hear. If someone is chattering away like that, you would probably just want to tell this so-called helper to shut up and help lift the piano. A real burden-bearer groans with you.[3]

And that, figuratively speaking, is what the Holy Spirit does for us when we pray. Equally wonderful is the fact that the Holy Spirit is completely in tune with the plans of God and knows exactly what God wants for us, and therefore what is best for us. As Paul writes, 'And he who searches our hearts knows the mind of the Spirit, because the Spirit intercedes for God's people in accordance with the will of God' (v. 27).

> Low at His feet lay thy burden of carefulness:
> High on His heart He will bear it for thee,
> Comfort thy sorrows and answer thy prayerfulness,
> Guiding thy steps as may best for thee be.[4]

FOR FURTHER READING: ROMANS 8:12–17, 26–34

Reflect on these points

1. *Jesus is telling us that the Holy Spirit is exactly the same as him, which is why we should always refer to the Holy Spirit as 'he' and not 'it'. He's a person, not a power.*

2. *Do you find prayer a problem? And maybe you also worry that you find prayer a problem. If we are God's children we should be reassured that the Bible tells us of truly godly people who struggled with not knowing what to pray for.*

3. *We are weak, but the Holy Spirit is all-powerful. He is completely in tune with the plans of God and knows exactly what God wants for us, and therefore what is best for us.*

Whose wisdom are you trusting?

Not many of you were wise by human standards ... But God *chose the foolish things of the world to shame the wise.*

(1 Cor. 1:26–27)

An American family moved to England and settled in Sheffield. Being sporty they decided to adopt a football team to support. When asked which team they were supporting they announced it was Sheffield United. Everyone's heart sank for them. The last time 'the Blades' won the FA Cup was 1925, and they haven't been English football champions since 1898. Oh well, as one football commentator wrote in their defence, 'Any team can have a bad century!', whilst someone else described them as 'a bunch of likable losers'. And when it comes to the Christian church, that is often how God's people are perceived. What is more, life in Corinth was all about winning, about being seen as influential and important. Corinthian life was all about the wise, the strong, the influential and those of noble birth. But in these verses, Paul shows us how God's way of choosing is the complete reverse of the world's. That was true in Corinth in Paul's day, and it is still true in today's church.

Indeed, it was true before Paul. The Old Testament is full of examples of God's deliberate choice of people who were the opposite of the ordinary standards of the world. In Deuteronomy, Moses writes of the children of Israel:

> The LORD did not set his affection on you and choose you because you were more numerous than other

peoples, for you were the fewest of all peoples. But it was because the Lord loved you ... (Deut. 7:7–8).

And this was reinforced by God's choosing Isaac over his older brother Ishmael, Jacob over his older twin Esau, and Ephraim over his older brother Manasseh. Then later, when Samuel was sent by God to Jesse's household to choose a king to succeed Saul, Samuel told Jesse, 'nor has the Lord chosen this one' when each of Jesse's seven eldest sons was presented. Then in the New Testament, Mary in her Magnificat sings of the God who has 'brought down rulers' and 'sent the rich away empty' but who has 'lifted up the humble' (Luke 1:51–53). And in his prayer, Jesus thanks his Father 'because you have hidden these things from the wise and learned, and revealed them to little children' (Matt. 11:25). As F. F. Bruce so magnificently puts it:

> Thus by the gospel, God annuls all conventional canons of wisdom, power, reputation and value. Nothing could be more subversive of the canons of first century Corinth than the proclamation of a crucified man exalted as Lord of the universe.[1]

Paul has been building an argument from verse 17. Christ sent me to preach the gospel, says Paul, 'not with words of eloquent wisdom, lest the cross of Christ be emptied of its power' (ESV). In contrast to the 'words of eloquent wisdom', Paul points out that 'the word of the cross' (v. 18, ESV) is 'foolishness to those who are perishing, but,' Paul adds, 'to us who are being saved it is the power of God'. In verse 21,

Paul notes how in his ministry God 'was pleased through the foolishness of what was preached to save those who believe'. What is more, 'the foolishness of God is wiser than human wisdom' (v. 25).

I suppose we should not be surprised, therefore, when an Anglican theologian—who gained a First in Classics from Oxford and later returned to complete a doctorate in Pauline theology, was then appointed Dean of Divinity at Magdalen College, and at the time of writing is Dean of one of England's cathedrals—states in a radio lecture that the idea of Christ taking the punishment for our sins on the cross is 'worse than illogical' and 'made God sound like a psychopath'.[2] No, not surprised; just saddened, because, put simply, 'Christ crucified' is not something that the world's academic elite, for all their vaunted scholarship, would ever have thought up. It's too simplistic, too unbelievable, too strange. As Dora Greenwell (1821–1882) wrote in the best-known of her hymns:

> I am not skilled to understand
> What God hath willed, what God hath planned;
> I only know at His right hand
> Stands One who is my Saviour.
>
> That He should leave His place on high
> And come for sinful man to die,
> You count it strange? So once did I
> Before I knew my Saviour.

So the poor spinster who lived mostly in obscurity, and

whose unadorned grave in Bristol receives no notice these days, understood what the Oxford Dean of Divinity did not. And so Paul writes to the Corinthians—and he says to each of us: just look at yourselves. 'Think of what you were when you were called' (v. 26). Just look around the church where you are. 'Not many of you were wise by human standards; not many were influential; not many were of noble birth. *But God* chose the foolish things of the world to shame the wise.' How relatively undistinguished were those Christians who assembled to hear Paul's letter read in comparison with the dazzling wealth and power of the elite of Corinth. And why is it that God chooses the Dora Greenwells—the likeable and even the unlikeable losers—of this world? 'So that no one may boast before him' (v. 29). Whose wisdom are you trusting— the wisdom of academia or the wisdom of God?

FOR FURTHER READING: 1 CORINTHIANS 1:17–31

Reflect on these points

1. *Life in Corinth was all about winning, about the wise, the strong, the influential and those of noble birth. But God's way of choosing is the complete reverse of the world's. That was true in Corinth in Paul's day, and it is still true today.*

2. *Why is it that God chooses the likeable and even the unlikeable losers of this world? 'So that no one may boast before him' (v. 29).*

3. *Whose wisdom are you trusting—the wisdom of academia or the wisdom of God?*

Reason or revelation?

'No eye has seen,
 nor ear has heard,
no mind has conceived
 what God has prepared for those who love him.'—
but God has revealed it to us by his Spirit.

(1 Cor. 2:9–10, NIV 1984)

In the opening chapter of his first letter to the Corinthians Paul has gone to great lengths to show that *worldly* wisdom is no use spiritually. Indeed, to the intellectual, Paul says, the gospel is utter foolishness. In saying this, he runs the risk of giving the impression that he's anti-intellectual. But it's rather like trying to undo half-truths. You spend so much time demolishing the lie that only after you've done that can you reinstate the bit that was true. Paul has been saying that human wisdom doesn't save you: human brain power won't make you a Christian. It's only once Paul has got that clear that he can tell us that Christians aren't credulous—we've got wisdom too.

And so in 2:6 Paul writes, 'We [that is, the apostles] do, however, speak a message of wisdom among the mature.' Now let's be clear: Paul is not advocating here a superior stage of Christian teaching reserved for some super-Christian elite. He makes it clear in verse 9 that these 'mature' Christians are those who truly 'love' God, and, in verse 12, that they are those who have received the Holy Spirit. But in verse 6, Paul contrasts this spiritual wisdom with the wisdom of this world. 'We speak wisdom,' he says, 'but not the wisdom of this age or of the rulers of this age, who are coming to nothing.' So what is 'the wisdom of this age'? It's what you will hear and read in the media from so-called opinion-formers, journalists, academics, the chattering classes, social commentators, and the likes of John Humphrys and Melvyn Bragg. But, says Paul, their so-called wisdom is a 'now' thing and it's coming to nothing.

In his book *In God We Doubt*, John Humphrys states that *if* God existed he would be 'exactly the sort of person you'd want your daughter to marry'.[1] Is it not an irony that when the so-called world-wise try to talk about spiritual things, they talk utter nonsense? An irony, yes, but, according to Paul, not a surprise. For in verse 7 Paul writes, 'No, we [the apostles] speak of God's secret wisdom, a wisdom that has been hidden' (NIV 1984). 'God's secret wisdom'—the Greek word is *musterio*, from which comes the English word 'mystery'. In biblical language a mystery is a previously hidden truth that has now been divinely revealed—that is, the Christian gospel. And why has God revealed it? 'For our glory,' says Paul in verse 7. And when did God conceive all this? 'God destined [it],' says Paul, 'for our glory *before time began*.' So the gospel is no afterthought; it's not a Plan B hastily put together because things did not work out quite as God had planned. No, the gospel is something planned in the mind of God from, literally, 'before the ages'. Remember too that unlike in our day, when new ideas and novelty are the vogue, in the ancient world of Corinth to whom Paul was writing it was antiquity that impressed, not novelty. So Paul is playing a trump card. 'You want antiquity?' he's saying. 'Well, how about wisdom that dates from before time began?'

But there's more, for Paul continues, 'None of the rulers of this age understood it, for if they had, they would not have crucified the Lord of glory' (v. 9). Pilate, Herod, Caiaphas— they knew what they were doing to Jesus in the human sense. They were going to have him crucified. But in the spiritual sense they were clueless. They didn't know that their evil butchery of Jesus would lead not only to their own undoing, but also to man's salvation. And it's so often the same today, as the world's rulers and power-brokers just cannot understand the Christian gospel.

And why not? Because, as Paul explains in verse 9, when it comes to God's plans and preparations, 'No eye has seen, no ear has heard, no mind has conceived what God has prepared' (NIV 1984). God's plans and preparations are, said John Stott, 'invisible, inaudible and inconceivable'.[2] Most commentators suggest that when Paul talks here about 'what God has prepared', he is harking back to those wonderful things he wrote of in verse 30 of the previous chapter—'righteousness, holiness and redemption'. And for whom has God prepared these things? For the worldly wise? No: for 'those who love [God]' (end of 2:9). And how do Paul and the apostolic band know all this? Because they reasoned it all out with their own intellectual skills? No, not through reason, but through revelation: 'No eye has seen, no ear has heard, no mind has

conceived what God has prepared for those who love him'—
but God has revealed it to us by his Spirit.'

> What kind of man is this
> Who died in agony?
> He who had done no wrong
> Was crucified for me.
> What kind of man is this
> Who laid aside His throne
> That I might know the love of God?
> What kind of man is this?
>
> By grace I have been saved;
> It is the gift of God.
> He destined me to be His son
> Such is His love.
> No eye has ever seen,
> No ear has ever heard,
> Nor has the heart of man conceived
> What kind of love is this.[3]

FOR FURTHER READING: 1 CORINTHIANS 2:1–10

Reflect on these points

1. *What is 'the wisdom of this age'? It's what you will hear and read in the media from so-called opinion-formers, journalists, academics, the chattering classes and social commentators. But their so-called wisdom is a 'now' thing and it's coming to nothing.*

2. *The gospel is no afterthought; it's not a Plan B hastily put together because things did not work out quite as God had planned. No, the gospel is something planned in the mind of God from 'before the ages'.*

3. *'Righteousness, holiness and redemption'—for whom has God prepared these things? For the worldly wise? No: for 'those who love' him.*

Great is thy faithfulness

No temptation has overtaken you except such as is common to man; but God is faithful ...

(1 Cor. 10:13, NKJV)

In his book *The Attributes of God*, Arthur W. Pink (1886–1952) writes that 'unfaithfulness is one of the most outstanding sins of these evil days'. He points to unfaithfulness in the business world, in marriage, even in the church, where 'thousands have solemnly promised to preach the truth [yet] make no scruple to attack and deny it'. He reminds us, too, of the many ways and times we have been unfaithful to God. 'How refreshing, then,' he writes, 'how unspeakably blessed, to lift our eyes above this scene of ruin, and behold One who *is* faithful, faithful in all things, faithful at all times.'[1]

The Bible is full of reminders of God's faithfulness. Moses records that at the second giving of the law on Mount Sinai,

> The LORD came down in the cloud and stood there with [Moses] and proclaimed his name ... 'The LORD, the LORD, the compassionate and gracious God, slow to anger, abounding in love and *faithfulness* (Exod. 34:5–6).

Later, Moses instructed Israel, 'Know therefore that the LORD your God is God; he is the *faithful* God' (Deut. 7:9). In the Psalms, David proclaims, 'Your love, LORD, reaches to the heavens, your *faithfulness* to the skies' (Ps. 36:5). The prophet Isaiah, looking forward to the coming of Christ, was inspired to write, 'Righteousness will be his belt and *faithfulness* the sash round his waist' (Isa. 11:5). And in the New Testament, Paul, writing to Timothy, tells him that even 'if we are faithless, he [God] remains *faithful*' (2 Tim. 2:13).

So what is the context of our text? Paul is using the history of Israel to teach us that there is such a thing as fake religion. He begins the chapter by summarizing the history of those who left Pharaoh's slavery in Egypt in the exodus and the journey to the land of promise, and he mentions the blessings they all enjoyed as they journeyed. In the first four verses he uses the word 'all' five times: '*all* our fathers were under the cloud, *all* passed through the sea, *all* were baptized into Moses ... *all* ate the same spiritual food, and *all* drank the same spiritual drink' (vv. 1–4, NKJV). But Paul then reminds us that 'God was not pleased with *most of them*' (v. 5), and all except Joshua and Caleb died in the wilderness. Most were not true people of faith: they were faking it.

Christians today are, as it were, reliving the experiences of our spiritual forefathers (v. 1). Redemption from the slavery in Egypt and the journey towards the Promised Land in the old covenant becomes redemption from the slavery of sin and death for the life journey towards God's kingdom in the new covenant. And just as the 'baptism' in the Red Sea and the 'spiritual food' and 'spiritual drink'—the manna and the water brought miraculously by God from the rock—were no guarantee of Israel's ultimate salvation, so baptism and the bread and wine of the Lord's Supper are no guarantees of our salvation. They don't make you a Christian. Just as, in the days of the exodus, being a physical member of the children of Israel did not save you, so today being a member of the visible church is no proof of membership of the invisible church of true believers. And 'these things ... were written down as warnings for us,' Paul tells the Corinthians (v. 11). So, Paul is saying to us, don't be presumptuous about salvation based on outward actions, rituals or membership.

Some of us, however, veer in the opposite direction. We are not presumptuous about gaining salvation: we are despairing about gaining salvation. Presumption is to believe what there is *no* good ground for believing. Despair is disbelieving what there *are* good grounds for believing. And it is to the despairing Christian that Paul turns in verse 13: 'No temptation has overtaken you except what is common to mankind,' he writes. The word rendered 'temptation' (*peirasmoi*) can also mean 'trials', and both, we are told, are part of general human experience. As Paul Barnett puts it, 'As fallen people in a fallen world we are all subject to moral temptation and prone to trying circumstances right through our lives.'[2]

'*But God ...*' '*But God* is faithful, who will not allow you to be tempted [or tried] beyond what you are able, but with the temptation [or trial] will also make the way of escape, that you may be able to bear it' (v. 13, NKJV). In temptation, 'the way of escape' may often be a good pair of heels, as we saw for Joseph in Chapter 4. Running from temptation is not cowardice, it's godly commonsense. In trials, it may mean, rather than praying, 'God, why have you let this happen to me?', praying

185

instead, 'God, what wonderful things are you going to teach me about yourself this time?' For God is always as good as his word, and in his Word he promises to those who are truly his, 'Never will I leave you; never will I forsake you' (Heb. 13:5). He has not promised to provide all our *wants*, but he has promised to provide all our *needs*. He is indeed one who is faithful in all things, and faithful at all times.

> Great is Thy faithfulness! Great is Thy faithfulness!
> Morning by morning new mercies I see;
> All I have needed Thy hand hath provided;
> Great is Thy faithfulness, Lord, unto me![3]

FOR FURTHER READING: 1 CORINTHIANS 10:1–13

Reflect on these points

1. Baptism and the bread and wine of the Lord's Supper are no guarantees of our salvation. They don't make you a Christian. And being a member of the visible church is no proof of membership of the invisible church of true believers. Paul is saying to us, don't be presumptuous about salvation based on outward actions, rituals or membership.

2. Some veer in the opposite direction: we are despairing about gaining salvation. Presumption is to believe what there is no good ground for believing. Despair is disbelieving what there are good grounds for believing.

3. In temptation, 'the way of escape' may often be a good pair of heels. In trials, it may mean, rather than praying,

'God, *why have you let this happen to me?*', *praying instead, 'God, what wonderful things are you going to teach me about yourself this time?*'

Christ is risen.
Hallelujah!

If only for this life we have hope in Christ, we are of all people most to be pitied. But Christ has indeed been raised from the dead.

(1 Cor. 15:19–20)

In his Easter hymn, the English cleric George Woodward (1848–1934) wrote movingly of Christians' Easter joy:

> This joyful Eastertide,
> Away with sin and sorrow!
> My Love, the Crucified,
> Hath sprung to life this morrow.

But he then reminds us of the centrality of Christ's resurrection to the Christian faith, putting into song some words from the fifteenth chapter of Paul's first letter to the Corinthians:

> Had Christ, that once was slain,
> Ne'er burst His three-day prison,
> Our faith had been in vain ...

In verse 12 of this chapter, Paul asks in astonishment, 'How can some of you say that there is no resurrection of the dead?' Clearly there was a significant faction of the Corinthian church that denied the whole idea of resurrection. In doing so, they were certainly blending in with the prevailing beliefs of their day, for neither the Greeks nor the Romans held any strong belief in immortality. Indeed, the inscription on tombstones reading '*non fui, fui, non sum, non desidero*' ('I was not. I was. I am not. I am free from wishes') was so common that it was often abbreviated to '*nffnsnd*'—in the same way as Christians came to abbreviate '*Requiescat In Pace*' ('May he/she rest in peace') to 'RIP'. But what were the Corinthian Christians thinking of in denying the resurrection? Paul lays out in lucid argument just what this would mean were it true.

As in Paul's day, this is a matter of 'first importance: that Christ died for our sins according to the Scriptures, that he was buried, that he was raised on the third day according to the Scriptures' (vv. 3–4). Judge David Turner QC tells of how a barrister once told him, 'It's when I have a really poor case that I make a really long speech. It's when I have a really strong case, I just call the witnesses.'[1] And 'call the witnesses' is what Paul does in verses 5–8: Peter, the Twelve, plus another five hundred, 'most of whom are still living'. Paul is writing around AD 56, less than thirty years after the resurrection. Would any of us seriously think we could get away with misrepresenting a major event of the 1990s?

Then Paul lays out in negative rhetoric five implications for the Christian if there is no resurrection. First, if there is no resurrection, the apostles' preaching is 'useless', and so is our faith (v. 14); or, as George Woodward, whom we quoted earlier, put it, 'our faith had been in vain'. It would all be bogus, worthless, nothing more than smoke and mirrors. '*But Christ* has indeed been raised from the dead,' says Paul (v. 20). Second, if there is no resurrection, the apostles would have been 'false witnesses' (v. 15). '*But Christ* has indeed been raised from the dead', which proves that what the apostles wrote is true and utterly reliable. In the resurrection, God proved Jesus to be true. Third, if there is no resurrection, and if Christ has not been raised, then 'you are still in your sins' (v. 17) and we would remain unforgiven. Paul puts this even more clearly in his letter to the Romans (4:25), where he writes that Jesus was 'delivered over to death for our sins and was raised to life for our justification'. The resurrection is God's affirmation—God's 'yes'—to Christ's work of salvation for us. So if there is no resurrection and if Christ did not rise, then the sin problem remains unresolved. '*But Christ* has indeed been raised from the dead.' Fourth, if there is no resurrection, then those who have died in Christ are 'lost' (v. 18) and there is no hope for them or for us. As someone once put it, 'Resurrection means an endless hope, but no resurrection means a hopeless end.' And so, fifth, says Paul, if there is no resurrection, 'we are of all people most to be pitied' (v. 19).

And then comes one of the great 'but's of the whole Bible: '*But Christ* has indeed been raised from the dead' (v. 20). Let's put Paul's negatives in the positive. Because Christ has been raised, our faith is well founded, the apostles' preaching is true, we are wholly forgiven, Christians who have died already are alive, and we are truly to be envied more than anyone else—all because there *is* a resurrection and Christ *has* been raised. As Archbishop Michael Ramsey (1904–1988) once expressed it, 'The gospel without a resurrection is not merely a gospel without a final chapter—it is not a gospel at all.'[2] If there is no resurrection, Christians would be making complete fools of themselves. But as the resurrection is true, we can echo the words of the Apostle Paul, 'But thanks be to God! He gives us the victory through our Lord Jesus Christ' (v. 57).

> Death's flood hath lost its chill,
> Since Jesus crossed the river:
> Lover of souls, from ill
> My passing soul deliver:
>
> *Had Christ that once was slain,*
> *Ne'er burst His three-day prison,*
> *Our faith had been in vain:*
> *But now hath Christ arisen,*
> *Arisen, arisen, arisen.*

Christ the Lord is risen indeed! Hallelujah!

FOR FURTHER READING: 1 CORINTHIANS 15

Reflect on these points

1. *If there is no resurrection, our faith would all be bogus, worthless, nothing more than smoke and mirrors.*

2. *If there is no resurrection, what the apostles wrote is untrue and utterly unreliable.*

3. *If there is no resurrection, we would remain in our sins and unforgiven.*

4. *If there is no resurrection, there is no hope for those who have died or for us.*

5. *If there is no resurrection, 'we are of all people most to be pitied'.*

6. *'But Christ has indeed been raised from the dead'!*

The gospel in two words

And you were dead in the trespasses and sins in which you once walked ... But God ... made us alive.

(Eph. 2:1–5, ESV)

A number of years ago, a society for the spread of atheism published a tract exposing the depravity of many of the great Bible heroes. Abraham, they noted, was a coward who was willing to sacrifice his wife's honour to save his own skin. It listed the verses where the Bible admits this, and then where the Bible calls him 'the friend of God'. 'What kind of God,' it then asked, 'would befriend so dishonourable a man?' Then there was Jacob, who, the tract noted, was a cheat and a liar; the tract asked, 'What does this say about the character of a God who would even call himself "the God of Jacob"?' Next came a reminder that Moses was a murderer, yet God chose him to bring his law to the world. And then there was David, who seduced Bathsheba and then had her husband killed to cover it up. 'Yet,' the tract complained, 'this is the man after God's own heart.'

So how would Christians answer these charges? Well, first by saying that everything the tract said is true! All the Bible heroes—excepting the Lord Jesus Christ—were sinful scoundrels and breakers of God's law, as indeed we all are. And that is exactly what the Apostle Paul lays out in the first three verses of the second chapter of Ephesians. Paul begins by saying that every one of us without God is spiritually dead. And the trouble with 'dead' is there's no room for comparisons or degrees. You can be good, better or best. You can be bad, worse or worst. But what you can't say is 'I'm dead, he's deader, she's deadest!' No, says Paul, you were dead—'in the trespasses and sins in which you once walked' (vv. 1–2, ESV), following the ways of the devil. It sounds bad. But it gets worse. Paul goes on to talk of living in 'the passions of our flesh' and 'the desires of the body and mind' (v. 3), with the result that we were 'children of [God's] wrath' (ESV).

'Now wait a minute,' I hear someone say, 'did you say *wrath*, *God's wrath*? Surely not.' Sadly, such a response is somewhat symptomatic of the problems Paul has been talking about in these preceding verses. For if we don't take sin seriously, we won't take a holy and righteous God's reaction to sin seriously. The theologian Jim Packer describes God's wrath as 'righteous anger—the right reaction of moral perfection in the Creator towards moral perversity in His creatures'. And he adds, 'so far from the manifestation of God's wrath in punishing sin being morally doubtful, the thing that *would* be morally doubtful would be for Him *not* to show His wrath against sin'.[1]

So that's the first three verses of the chapter. Have we the stomach to read on? Well, there are only two words that could get me to read on—in hope. They are the first two words of verse 4—'*But God*': what the American commentator R. C. Sproul has called his two most favourite words in all the Bible. Yes, we were dead, '*but God* ... made us alive together with Christ' (vv. 4–5, ESV). And how has he done that? Through his mercy (v. 4), his great love (v. 4), his grace (v. 5) and his kindness (v. 7). That's four ways of saying much the same thing. But notice that all the initiative is God's. It's *God's* mercy, *God's* love, *God's* grace and *God's* kindness.

And here's something else we may not be entirely comfortable about: that there's nothing I can bring to my salvation; that it's *all* of God's grace. We're uncomfortable about this if in our heart of hearts we really believe, not in the gospel according to Jesus Christ, but in the gospel according to Julie Andrews. Let me explain. If you've ever watched the classic 1965 film *The Sound of Music* you will probably remember the scene after Maria (Julie Andrews) and Captain von Trapp (Christopher Plummer) have fallen in love and they're alone, in the summer house, and Julie Andrews sings,

> For here you are, standing there, loving me,
> Whether or not you should,
> So somewhere in my youth or childhood,
> I must have done something good.

Well, it may be very sweet, but it's not grace! For grace brings good without it being deserved—without 'somewhere in my youth or childhood' having 'done something good'. But the trouble comes when we bring a *Sound of Music* mindset to our thinking about God. We'll accept that we are saved by grace, but surely God won't deny his grace to those who have 'done their best'. And so we end up believing in Grace-Plus— grace plus doing our best.

So what has God done for us? We are no longer dead, but alive; no longer slaves of sin, but sons of God; no longer under

God's wrath, but beneficiaries of God's grace—and all this through Christ alone, by grace alone.

> Nothing in my hand I bring;
> Simply to Thy cross I cling;
> Naked, come to Thee for dress,
> Helpless, look to Thee for grace;
> Foul, I to the fountain fly;
> Wash me, Saviour, or I die.[2]

Have you prayed that prayer? Can you give testimony to the fact that, once you were weighed down by the burden of your sin, *but God* has washed you in the precious blood of Christ? Have you had a 'but God' moment in your life? 'And you were dead in the trespasses and sins in which you once walked … *But God* … made [you] alive.' '*But God* …' It's the gospel in two words.

FOR FURTHER READING: EPHESIANS 2:1–9

Reflect on these points

1. *Every one of us without God is spiritually dead. And the trouble with 'dead' is there's no room for comparisons or degrees.*

2. *If we don't take sin seriously, we won't take a holy and righteous God's reaction to sin seriously.*

3. *Maybe we are not entirely comfortable about the fact that there's nothing I can bring to my salvation; that it's all of God's grace. Surely God won't deny his grace to*

those who have 'done their best'? And so we end up believing in Grace-Plus—grace plus doing our best.

4. *Can you give testimony to the fact that, once you were weighed down by the burden of your sin, but God has washed you in the precious blood of Christ? Have you had a 'but God' moment in your life?*

Epilogue

The eminent preacher and writer John Stott (1921–2011) wrote that 'These two monosyllables—"but God"—set against the desperate condition of fallen mankind the gracious initiative and sovereign action of God.'[1] Indeed, these two words show what God has done and continues to do for us. If we are truly followers of the Lord Jesus Christ, this should greatly encourage us in our daily walk with him. Have I been the victim of other people's sin and ill will? I can say, 'You intended to harm me, *but God* intended it for good' (Gen. 50:20). Do I feel threatened? *But God* watches over me (Ezra 5:5). Have I yet again fallen into sin? *But God*, like a loving father, is full of compassion and mercy towards me, and freely forgives me (Luke 15:20). Do I feel that God is distant and hidden from view? *But Jesus* has made him known (John 1:18). Do I struggle with prayer? *But the Holy Spirit* intercedes for me (Rom. 8:26). Am I beset by temptations? *But God* is faithful, and provides me with a way of escape (1 Cor. 10:13). Was I not once dead in my sins? *But God* has made me alive in Christ (Eph. 2:4–5). If this is indeed your experience, then I trust that these short studies will have made you want to echo the psalmist's words: 'Return to your rest, my soul, for the LORD has been good to you' (Ps. 116:7).

On the other hand, if you have yet to give God his rightful place on the throne of your life and are still trying to hide from or ignore him, these two words—'but God'—may trouble you, and rightly so. For you have also seen that the Scriptures say that you may be trying to hide from God, *but God* will find you and question you (Gen. 3:8–9). You may be trying to put off allowing God to rule your life, *but Christ* tells you to come and follow him now (Matt. 8:22). You may be trying to deceive God—and yourself—by claiming to live a 'good life'. *But Jesus* knows your hypocrisy (Mark 12:15). You may be living merely for the present and for pleasure, with no thought of God at all. *But Jesus* says, 'You fool!' (Luke 12:20). If in a moment of unvarnished honesty you realize that this is your current state, then I urge you, before you put this book down for the last time, to look more closely at the passage from Ephesians on which our final study was based:

> And you were *dead in the trespasses and sins in which you once walked*, following the course of this world, following the prince of the power of the air, the spirit that is now at work in the sons of disobedience—among whom we all once lived in the passions of our flesh, carrying out the desires of the body and the mind, and were by nature *children of wrath*, like the rest of mankind. But God, being rich in mercy, because of the great love with which he loved us, even when we were dead in our trespasses, *made us alive* together with Christ … so that in the coming ages he might show the immeasurable riches of his grace in kindness towards us in Christ Jesus. For *by grace* you have been saved through faith. And this is *not your own doing*; it is the

gift of God, not a result of works, so that no one may boast (Eph. 2:1–9, ESV).

Let us briefly ask three questions about these verses. First, what is our spiritual state before we turn to Christ? We are 'dead in the trespasses and sins in which [we] once walked'. We are spiritually like corpses—unable to seek God or even to respond to him. And because of God's righteous anger at our sin, we are 'children of [God's] wrath'. We deserve to be punished for our sin.

But, second, what has God done for us? We were spiritually dead, but God has 'made us alive'. Through his death on the cross, Jesus paid the price for our sin, and only he who had lived a perfect, sinless life could do that. As the Good Friday hymn puts it so clearly,

> There was no other good enough
> To pay the price of sin;
> He *only* could unlock the gate
> Of heaven, and let us in.[2]

And if we 'trust in His redeeming blood', God gives us eternal life in Christ. Then we are no longer spiritually dead but alive, and physical death will have no lasting hold on us. As Jesus tells us, 'I am the resurrection and the life. The one who believes in me will live, even though they die' (John 11:25). As Jesus then said to Martha, 'Do you believe this?' (v. 26).

But, third, why has God done this? This is the most amazing part of it all and these verses from Ephesians give us the answer.

First, the negative part: 'This is not your own doing,' says Paul (Eph. 2:8); and, he adds, it is 'not a result of works' (v. 9)—it is not anything we do. So why has God done this? 'Because of the great *love* with which he loved us,' says Paul, and because he 'is rich in *mercy*' (v. 4). It is 'by *grace* you have been saved' (v. 5). Love, mercy and grace!

> Amazing grace! How sweet the sound,
> That saved a wretch like me!
> I once was lost, but now am found;
> Was blind, but now I see.[3]

Or, as Francis Rowley puts it in his hymn, 'I was lost, *but Jesus* found me'![4] If you want to understand more of what this means, I urge you to get hold of a modern translation of the Bible (both the *New International Version* and the *English Standard Version* are excellent) and sit down and read through Mark's Gospel. It will be only about twenty-five pages long. Before you read, pray that God, through his Holy Spirit, would reveal to you the truths of his holy Word. For truly, '"no eye has seen, no ear has heard, no mind has conceived what God has prepared for those who love him"—*but God* has revealed it to us by his Spirit' (1 Cor. 2:9–10, NIV, 1984).

Endnotes

Foreword

1   James Montgomery Boice, *Genesis: An Expositional Commentary*, Vol. 3 (Grand Rapids, MI: Baker, 2006), p. 1252.

2   R. C. Sproul, *Ephesians: The Purpose of God* (Fearn: Christian Focus, 2011), pp. 51–52.

3   James Montgomery Boice, *Ephesians* (Grand Rapids, MI: Baker, 1988), p. 54.

4   Francis H. Rowley, 'I Will Sing the Wondrous Story' (1886).

Ch. 1 God's first question

1   All emphasis in Scripture quotes has been added by the author.

2   Peter Williams, *Jonah: Running From God. An Expositional Commentary, Exploring the Bible* (Epsom: Day One, 2003), p. 95.

3   William O. Cushing, 'Oh, Safe to the Rock That Is Higher Than I' (1876).

Ch. 2 Remembering

1   'General Thanksgiving', *Book of Common Prayer* (1662).

2   Timothy Dudley-Smith, 'O God, Whose All-Sustaining Hand' (1997).

Ch. 3 God sees

1   Thomas Ken, 'Awake, My Soul, and With the Sun' (1695).

2   Thomas B. Pollock, 'We Have Not Known Thee As We Ought' (1889).

Ch. 4 God with us

1   Quoted in Jonathan Aitken, *Charles W. Colson: A Life Redeemed* (London: Continuum, 2005), p. 268.

2   Iain M. Duguid, *Living in the Light of Inextinguishable Hope: The Gospel According to Joseph* (Phillipsburg, NJ: P&R, 2013), p. 57.

Ch. 5 My weakness ... God's strength

1   Charles Colson, *Kingdoms in Conflict* (Grand Rapids, MI: Zondervan, 1987), pp. 306–307.

2   Thoro Harris, 'Who Can Cheer the Heart Like Jesus?' (1931).

Ch. 6 God's perfect plan

1 Henry Blunt, *A Family Exposition of the Pentateuch*, Vol. 3 (London: Hatchard, 1851), p. 29.

2 John Newton, *Out of the Depths: An Autobiography* (Chicago: Moody Press), p. 8.

Ch. 7 Looking back … looking forward

1 Charles Haddon Spurgeon, 'Four Choice Sentences', in *Metropolitan Tabernacle Pulpit*, Vol. 27 (1882; repr. London: Banner of Truth, 1971), p. 647; quoted in James Montgomery Boice, *Genesis: An Expositional Commentary*, Vol. 3 (Grand Rapids, MI: Baker, 1998), p. 1173.

2 Stuart Townend and Keith Getty, 'O Church, Arise'. Copyright © 2005 Thankyou Music.

Ch. 8 God working for our good

1 'Confession, Holy Communion (First Order)', *An English Prayer Book* (Church Society, 1994).

Ch. 9 Not judging by appearances

1 Dale Ralph Davis, *1 Samuel: Looking on the Heart* (Fearn: Christian Focus, 2000), p. 170.

2 Charles Wesley, 'O for a Heart to Praise My God' (1742).

Ch. 10 God's watchful eye

1 *'Spero infestis, metuo secundis'*—on Henry Blunt's memorial tablet, Holy Trinity Church, Sloane Square, London.

2 Tiberius Rata, *Ezra and Nehemiah: A Mentor Commentary* (Fearn: Christian Focus, 2010), p. 77.

3 Isaac Watts, 'Had Not the Lord, May Israel Say' (1719).

Ch. 11 A question of life or death

1 Isaac Watts (1709).

Ch. 12 Excuses! Excuses!

1 A. A. Milne, *Winnie-the-Pooh* (London: Methuen & Co, 1926), p. 48.

2 Philip Graham Ryken, *Jeremiah and Lamentations: From Sorrow to Hope* (Wheaton, IL: Crossway, 2001), p. 22.

3 Frank Houghton, 'Facing a Task Unfinished' (1931).

Ch. 13 A wind, a 'whale' and a worm

1 William Banks, *Jonah: The Reluctant Prophet* (Chicago: Moody Press, 1966), p. 20.

2 Robert Robinson, 'Come, Thou Fount of Every Blessing' (1758).

3 Frederick W. Faber, 'There's a Wideness in God's Mercy' (1862).

Ch. 14 Godly priorities

1 Dietrich Bonhoeffer, *The Cost of Discipleship* (London: SCM Press, 2015), p. 4.

Ch. 15 Peace in the storm

1 The Revd Dr John C. Harper, Rector of St John's Church, Lafayette Square, Washington DC, in his Good Friday Addresses, 'In the Cross of Christ I Glory', 9 April 1993.

2 R. Kent Hughes, *Mark: Jesus, Servant and Savior* (Wheaton, IL: Crossway, 2015), p. 114.

3 John Newton, 'Though Troubles Assail' (1779).

Ch. 16 From 'Mission Impossible' to 'Mission Accomplished'

1 'Christians Must Stand Up for Their Faith in a Secular Society', *Times Educational Supplement*, 29 January 2016.

2 John Eddison, 'At the Cross of Jesus' (1942).

Ch. 17 Jesus knows

1 At the time of writing, Nigel Farage was the former leader of the United Kingdom Independence Party (UKIP) and Jean-Claude Juncker was President of the European Commission.

2 Joseph M. Scriven, 'What a Friend We Have in Jesus' (1855).

Ch. 18 A healing faith

1 Charles Wesley, 'Depth of Mercy! Can There Be' (1740).

Ch. 19 'You fool!'

1 William Cowper, 'O for a Closer Walk with God' (1772).

Ch. 20 The parable of the prodigal father

1 Philip G. Ryken, *Luke*, Vol. 2 (Phillipsburg, NJ: P&R, 2009), p. 146.

Ch. 21 Silence that is *not* golden

1 Emily M. Crawford, 'Speak, Lord, in the Stillness' (1920).

Ch. 22 The unique Christ

1 Quoted in Joan Biskupic, *American Original: The Life and Constitution of Antonin Scalia* (New York: Farrar, Straus & Giroux, 2009), p. 25.

2 John Stott, 'The Word to Make God Plain', Sermon preached at All Souls, Langham Place, London, 1 January 2006.

3 C. S. Lewis, *Mere Christianity*, quoted in Jonathan Gould, *What Christians Believe* (Fearn: Christian Focus, 2012), pp. 79–80.

Ch. 23 I know that my Redeemer lives!

1 Cecil Frances Alexander, 'There Is a Green Hill Far Away' (1848).

2 Stuart Townend, 'How Deep the Father's Love For Us' © 1995 Thankyou Music.

3 Samuel Medley, 'I Know That My Redeemer Lives' (1775).

Ch. 24 How do I know God loves me?

1 R. C. Sproul, *Romans: The Gospel of God* (Fearn: Christian Focus, 2011), p. 120.

2 William Walsham How, 'It Is a Thing Most Wonderful' (1872).

Ch. 25 Sin's wages … God's gift

1 Horatius Bonar, 'Not What These Hands Have Done' (1861).

Ch. 26 The burden-bearer

1 Henry Francis Lyte, 'Praise, My Soul, the King of Heaven' (1834).

2 Quoted in R. Kent Hughes, *Romans: Righteousness from Heaven* (Wheaton, IL: Crossway, 2013), p. 156.

3 James Montgomery Boice, *Romans: The Reign of Grace* (Grand Rapids, MI: Baker, 1992), p. 890.

4 John Samuel Bewley Monsell, 'O Worship the Lord in the Beauty of Holiness' (1863).

Ch. 27 Whose wisdom are you trusting?

1 F. F. Bruce, *1 and 2 Corinthians* (London: Marshall, Morgan & Scott, 1971), p. 36.

2 Jeffrey John in BBC *Lent Talks*, 4 April 2007.

Ch. 28   Reason or revelation?

1   John Humphrys, *In God We Doubt: Confessions of a Failed Atheist* (London: Hodder & Stoughton, 2007), pp. 4–5.

2   John Stott, 'The Spirit and the Bible', Sermon preached at All Souls, Langham Place, London, 9 March 1980.

3   Bryn and Sally Hayworth, 'What Kind of Love Is This?' © 1983 Signalgrade/Bella Music.

Ch. 29   Great is thy faithfulness!

1   Arthur W. Pink, *The Attributes of God* (Grand Rapids, MI: Baker, 1975), p. 66.

2   Paul Barnett, *1 Corinthians: Holiness and Hope for a Rescued People* (Fearn: Christian Focus, 2011), pp. 175–176.

3   Thomas O. Chisholm, 'Great is Thy Faithfulness' (1923).

Ch. 30   Christ is risen. Hallelujah!

1   David Turner, 'Why Is the Resurrection Good News?', Sermon preached at All Souls, Langham Place, London, 18 January 2009.

2   Quoted by Turner, ibid.

Ch. 31   The gospel in two words

1   J. I. Packer, *Knowing God* (London: Hodder & Stoughton, 1973), p. 167.

2   Augustus M. Toplady, 'Rock of Ages, Cleft for Me' (1775).

Epilogue

1   John R. W. Stott, *God's New Society: The Message of Ephesians* (Downers Grove, IL: Inter-Varsity Press, 1979), pp. 79–80; quoted in James Montgomery Boice, *Ephesians: An Expositional Commentary* (Grand Rapids, MI: Baker, 2006), p. 54.

2   Cecil Frances Alexander, 'There Is a Green Hill' (1848).

3   John Newton, 'Amazing Grace!' (1779).

4   Francis H. Rowley, 'I Will Sing the Wondrous Story' (1886).